EXPLORING POETRY OF PRESENCE II

PRAISE FOR THIS BOOK

"If you long to walk more deeply into the wilderness of poetry, I can't think of a more masterful and generous guide than poet Rosemerry Wahtola Trommer. In this companion edition, Rosemerry takes you by the hand and leads you to closer intimacy with not only poetry, but with all of life."

Julia Fehrenbacher,
poet and author of *Staying in Love*

∾

"Rosemerry Wahtola Trommer has always been a wise and gentle guide, leading us into deeper presence with her luminous poems. Yet what she has crafted here, as a companion to an already soul-nourishing anthology, is nothing short of a sacred text that will lift you up, and keep you company on the whole human journey—from joy to loss and back to the joy of full aliveness again."

James Crews,
author of *Kindness Will Save the World*

EXPLORING POETRY OF PRESENCE II

PROMPTS TO DEEPEN YOUR WRITING PRACTICE

ROSEMERRY WAHTOLA TROMMER

Foreword by
PHYLLIS COLE-DAI & RUBY R. WILSON

BACK PORCH PRODUCTIONS LLC

ISBN: 978-1-7371055-3-4

For information write to the publisher:
Back Porch Productions LLC, 46855 200th St., Bruce SD 57220-5210

Visit the author's website: wordwoman.com

Author photograph credit: Joanie Schwarz

for Mom

NOTE TO THE READER

The twin intentions of this companion guidebook are to enrich your experience of *Poetry of Presence II* and to deepen your writing of poetry as a mindfulness practice. The book extends eighty-eight invitations to write while drawing upon every poem in the anthology at least once.

All page numbers in the text refer to *Poetry of Presence II*, which you will want to have at hand. Sources for quotations beyond the anthology appear in the endnotes.

May your exploration of poetry take you where you've never been.

CONTENTS

FOREWORD

Happy warning: This book is likely to transform your life.

Poetry can do that, you know. Reading it. Writing it. Sharing it.

So can the wise guidance of a gifted poet like Rosemerry Wahtola Trommer.

If this book happens to be your introduction to the Word Woman, be aware: once she has entered your door, you'll want her to stay. She gets the power of words. She gets the joy of joining heart to pen, pen to page, page to breath, breath to world. She gets how engagement with poetry can be an intensely spiritual, as well as literary, practice.

Like Gloria Heffernan, who created a marvelous volume to companion your exploration of the original *Poetry of Presence*, Rosemerry has provided a living text to facilitate your poetry reading and writing. All you have to do now is show up.

Phyllis Cole-Dai & Ruby R. Wilson
Editors, *Poetry of Presence II*

INTRODUCTION

Consider this an invitation to join the big conversation—the conversation happening across cultures, across continents, across centuries—in which every poem ever written contributes to our understanding of this question: *What does it mean to be alive?*

In this book, we're specifically conversing with the poems in *Poetry of Presence II: An Anthology of Mindfulness Poems,* poems the editors chose for their ability "to crack open the tough stuff and spill out the light." You'll want to have that book on hand to use this book. The editors, Ruby R. Wilson and Phyllis Cole-Dai, selected poems that invite us to "practice mindfulness smack dab in the middle of our busy lives where we have hungry babies to feed, groceries to buy, a day's labor to perform, bills to pay, illnesses to endure, relationships to repair, injustices to remedy . . ."[1]

Beyond choosing poems that bring mindfulness into daily life, they also selected poems that "delve into varieties of suffering: woundedness, illness, loss, and death; prejudice, bigotry, injustice; violence and war." In other words, in this book we're going to converse with poems that ask us to meet things we'd sometimes prefer to shy away from.

I'm grateful that Phyllis and Ruby brought the mindfulness

conversation into the melee of daily life and global struggles. This is a conversation I want to be a part of—you, too?

~

Four Ways to Write Poems
(or Other Kinds of Writing)
Inspired by *Poetry of Presence II*

There are many ways to converse with these poems.

- Choose any line in any poem that stands out to you. Write it down. Begin there. Credit the original poet in your own poem by adding a line below your title that says, "with a line by (_____)" and then naming their poem in quotation marks. You can also choose to credit them with an epigraph, as Christen Careaga does in "Forgiveness" (91).

- Write a response to the poet, a poem in the form of a letter, that argues or agrees with their poem.

- Write a "cento" that takes lines from different poems. Cut them apart and weave them together in new ways. At the end of the poem, cite your source material in a "gloss"—basically, a list of footnotes. But a gloss is more than scholarly citing. As poet Gloria Heffernan writes, "it is a compilation of gratitude . . . a roadmap back to a special place." [2]

- Use this book's invitations to write, all of them inspired by the poems in *Poetry of Presence II*. Start at the beginning or flip around. If the prompts don't work for you, change them! Do what rises in you to do.

~

Writing as a Mindfulness Practice

This book is more than an invitation to write poems. It's a chance to explore writing as a mindfulness *practice*. The invitations to write are less oriented toward producing something *good* and more oriented toward sparking curiosity about process and how you connect with the world. What happens when you show up to the moment with a pen in your hand?

But isn't the point to write something good?

I hope not.

In my experience, when I sit down to write something *good*, I shut down. I get critical, frustrated and stuck—pretty much the opposite of mindfulness. But! Imagine a writing practice in which we become increasingly accepting, compassionate and open.

It's possible. I realized this back in 2006 when I began writing a poem every day, a practice that sustains and nourishes me still. To be honest, mindfulness was not my original goal. I just wanted to write good poems. Very quickly I realized I couldn't write a "masterpiece" every day. But if writing good poems wasn't the point, what was?

Writing anything can change the way we meet the world, but this may be especially true when we write poetry. First, it can change how we move through a day. Perhaps you have noticed this, too—how knowing you will write a poem makes you more open to the world around you as you look for inspiration. In those first months, even years, of daily poeming, I was grateful for the ways I was always looking for the poems. It made me pay attention more to everything—both what was happening around me and what was happening inside me.

Second, writing poems can help us realize we have the power to frame things—and to reframe them, and to reframe them again. Here's an example. One night I wrote a poem about how I was a vase, and I was becoming a bigger and bigger vase to hold everything, to hold it all. It felt very true. Then, the next day, I was speaking about it with my spiritual teacher Joi Sharp, and she asked, "Are you sure you need to hold it?"[3] And just like that, the frame changed. That day I wrote a poem about being porous, like a sieve, allowing everything in the world to move through me with no need for me to hold it. Such a powerful reframing. To write a poem is to be able to change the way we conceive of the world and how we meet it.

I have come to see the poems as artifacts—the happy byproduct of the *real* practice, which is being open to what is here, saying yes to the world as it is, telling the truth the best we can in that moment. That's not to say the poems don't matter. They do! Poems can save lives, mine included. They bring pleasure. They provoke us. They challenge us. They change us. I have thousands (truly!) of books filled with poems I love to read. I've dedicated my life to reading and writing and sharing poems.

But the words themselves are not what's really at stake. They are the proverbial fingers pointing at the moon. When we put the practice first, then the dark and light come pouring in and we are stunned by our own aliveness.

❧

Four Promises for a Mindful Writing Practice

As my practice evolved, I arrived at a set of four promises for myself that I now use each time I sit down to write—promises that infuse my writing with the principles of mindfulness. Maybe you'll appreciate them, too. The invitations in them feel equally true whether you write every day or only once in your life.

Promise #1: *I will write.*

Well. That's easy. Maybe I only write a sentence. Maybe I write fifty lines of poetry. It doesn't matter. The promise just means that I will show up with a pen (or keyboard) and something will happen.

People often say to me, "You must have to write." No. It's the easiest thing in the world *not* to write. Choosing to write anything takes discipline. Sometimes, of course, the words just pour out—you've likely experienced this, too. But what about when they don't? That doesn't mean there's not something to be gained from sitting with a blank piece of paper.

There was a time when I was afraid of the blank. It felt like a challenge. Like an *opponent*. Now, I love sitting with blank, sometimes for a very long time. I love when blank rubs off on me. It's a beautiful way to enter a relationship with quietude, with stillness, with openness. Eventually I trust the writing will come. And every day, for seventeen years, that's been true.

But there are other ways to do this practice right. I remember hearing an interview with Jane Hirshfield in which she said she shows up to write every day, but if no words come, that's okay with her. She knows she'll come back to the page the next day.

You will know what's right for you in your practice. Perhaps writing nothing is exactly right for you today. Perhaps you write fifteen poems. If you show up, you can only do this right.

Promise #2: *It doesn't have to be good, but it has to be true.*

This was the biggest breakthrough in my relationship with writing poetry. It changed everything. If I had to write something good, then I failed every time. But *I will write something true* is a promise I can keep every time. In every poem, I ask myself again and again: *What's the next true thing? What's the next true thing?* And in this way, a poem is written.

By *true*, I don't necessarily mean factual. I can write a poem that is true about channeling my inner dragon or inner dodo. My promise to myself means I don't want to write to be clever or to impress someone else. There must be real juice in the writing, real energy.

The irony? I've found when I write something true, it has resonance. And someone else reads it and says, "Oh, yes! I know that! That's good!"

Promise #3: *I can't know the end when I start.*

Why not?

I've come to learn that a mindful writing practice is most alive when I let the writing know more than I do. When I know the ending at the start, I cut myself off from any epiphany, any surprise. Writing becomes an act of reporting, not an act of discovery.

But what if you already know the end? Of course, this happens. In these cases, I force myself to write past the ending I already know. Or, I write the ending I already know and then chop it off and write another. And another. And another.

I happen to love this endings exercise and highly recommend you play often: Take any line from any poem in *Poetry of Presence II*. Use it as the first line of a two-line poem. Now you write the second line. Once you've done this, do it again. Use the same first line, but then write a *new* two-line poem by changing the ending. And do it again. Do it ten times. Thirty. What you will discover is that there are so many ways to end a poem "right." So many possible very satisfying endings! So often, we get caught up in thinking there is only one way to do it right—that we are supposed to end up at the right ending for our poem. Ha! This little poetry game teaches me possibility, openness, potential, curiosity, abundance, nonattachment, and so many other facets of mindfulness.

But, said one of my students, "Can't I know the end and find infinite paths to get there?" Um, yeah! Just as there are many possible ways to get to Helsinki from here, the epiphanies and surprises might come from the journey we choose to get there. I would say this: What is most important when writing as a mindfulness practice is putting ourselves in service to what we're writing, in letting ourselves be led by *I don't know.*

As my beloved friend Jack Mueller used to say of writing poetry, "Obey the poem's emerging form."

Promise #4: *I will share.*

Really? Is that necessary?

Well, friend, here's how I see it. It's like breathing. When we participate in writing as a mindfulness practice, we are taking in the world, and taking in the world, and taking in the world. Noticing and paying attention and being present. It's like a never-ending inhale. And to write and share what we've written is the exhale. It's what keeps the process sustainable.

Do you have to share everything you write? No. Do you have to make it public? No. Do you have to put your name on it? No. Do you have to publish it? No. So many ways to do it right! Perhaps you show it to a friend. Perhaps you have a conversation about it. Perhaps you send it to the author with whom your writing is conversing. Perhaps you leave it in a book at the library for someone else to find. Perhaps you find one or two other people who are also writing, and you agree to exchange work, reading each other's writing not for critique but for conversation.

I believe what poet and ritual leader Kim Rosen says about our relationship to poems and each other: "We come to poetry for moments of truth. We share it with others for moments of communion."[4] This gets to the heart of why I thrill in joining my small voice to the big conversation—it's communion.

❧

What's at Stake

If you choose to explore writing as a mindfulness practice, chances are it will change a lot more than your writing. A consistent mindful writing practice has opened me, softened me, and made me more willing to be vulnerable, more invested in honesty, more embracing of paradox and more trusting of life. I feel a spaciousness and generosity and peace I didn't know before—even when in the presence of trauma, loss, fear and woundedness. *This* is why this practice matters.

In 2021 my son chose to take his own life. There are many "right" ways to meet great loss. For me, in that moment, and in many moments since, I have been grateful for an ability and deep desire to be open to life, to love and to connection while I am amidst "the tough stuff." I find myself turning again and again and again toward an impossibly great hurt and meeting it without shutting down. I believe this is possible because, when the stakes were lower, I cultivated a practice of presence, showing up every day and asking *What is here? What is true right now? How can I be available to this moment?*

A mindful poetry practice can be an unexpectedly generous gift to ourselves. We need not bring wisdom. We need not bring talent. We need not bring skills. All we are asked to bring is our willingness to show up with a blank piece of paper and a pen and let ourselves be led by the next true thing. Oh, and it doesn't hurt to show up with another poem as a guide. That's what this book is all about.

THE INVITATIONS

PAYING ATTENTION

This is where all poetry begins—with a willingness to notice the world around us and the world inside us. What is the outer landscape? What do you see, smell, taste, touch and hear? What is the inner landscape? What do you feel, think and wonder? Mindfulness poems build a bridge between these two worlds.

And yet, there's this: No matter how much we pay attention, the truths of the world will slip through our hands. I love the homage to humanness in "Dust" by Dorianne Laux (41), in which the speaker of the poem, out of exhaustion, is unable to recall a profound truth. The invitation, then, is to embrace our imperfection and stay "rapt, aware," at least to the best of our ability, as we continue to move through the world.

≈

What Finds You Today?

Invitation to Read

One of the easiest kinds of poems to write is the list poem. Imagine how many lists you've made! Why not use this skill for writing poems? Consider how "It Could Be," by Julia M. Fehrenbacher (28), uses a repeated line, "It could be . . ." to create a list of things that, by the end of the poem, remind the speaker (and reader) of something important, something known. One of the keys to a mindfulness poem practice can be to let ourselves be immersed in the details of the world, and in this poem, Fehrenbacher includes every sense, naming things happening *outside* the body. But by the end of the poem, we arrive at a revelation *inside* the body.

Invitation to Write

Write your own list poem of what "finds you" today. What do you notice happening in the world around you in this moment? Use as many senses as seem reasonable. You can use Fehrenbacher's phrase, "It could be ____ " as a refrain and fill in that blank again and again. For instance, "It could be the snow falling in thick white flakes." As you continue to make your list, see if something starts to show up inside you in response to all these external stimuli. Go there. Let the outer world lead you to the inner world. If nothing shows up, don't force it. Write about what doesn't show up. Or write a longing for something to show up. Whatever you do, write something true.

～

"Can You Hear It?"

Invitation to Read

Some days, like the one described above, the world just seems to find us, through no effort of our own. Other days, we are "simply blind to what the world has to offer," as Paula Lepp writes in "Can You Hear It?" (31). What do we do then? Perhaps this: Think small. I love how Lepp's poem shows how we might turn to the smallest thing, perhaps the grass beneath our feet, and offer it our attention. And then, as Lepp does, we might lower our expectations for what revelation or insight might come. Perhaps there's no gong of clarity. Perhaps we hear only "faint little bell-notes of joy." Sometimes that small tinkling is all it takes to bring us totally into the present.

Invitation to Write

Go in search of something, anything, to offer your attention. I promise anything will work: Natural. Manufactured. Beautiful. Repulsive. *Anything.* Be with it. Make a list of its attributes. Then make a list of its uses or what it does. Just making these lists often helps me pay better attention. Then ask the object, "What do you have to teach me?" And "really listen," as Lepp says, a kind of full-body listening. Perhaps you intuit an answer. Perhaps you don't. Either of these experiences is equally interesting to explore—receiving wisdom from the world or longing to receive wisdom from the world. Write about this experience.

∽

OTHER POEMS THAT SPEAK TO PAYING ATTENTION:

"What It's Like to Fall in Love," Heidi Seaborn, 30.
"Dust," Dorianne Laux, 41.

FINDING OUR STARTING PLACE

Where do we start? The process of writing can help us bring our heads and hearts to where our bodies are, inviting us to return to the present moment again and again. Any moment can be an entry point. "You begin where you do without knowing how," writes Phyllis Cole-Dai in "You Are a Poem with Feet" (178). Such a beautiful permission this line offers us. We need not wait until we know something—the poem waiting to be written is inviting us to begin now, wherever we are. What if you sit right now and just begin to write? What will emerge?

∾

Start at the End

Invitation to Read

There's nothing like an ending to teach us about beginnings. "In Love Elegy with Busboy" (42), Nathan McClain describes the aftermath in a restaurant where a table is left with both a literal mess after a meal and an emotional mess after a "reckless" conversation. But once the table is carefully cleared and replaced, McClain breathes possibility into what seems so certain: "Who's to say we can't start over, if we want?"

Invitation to Write

Write a poem in which you describe how something ended—a relationship or a dream or story you told yourself. Set the scene, or as my old fiction professor James Yaffe used to say, "Get the weather right." Try to tell it as a witness, without attachment to right or wrong. Just the facts. Perhaps write it in third person for additional distance.

Now ask questions of the ending of the dream or relationship or story, as if you are interviewing it. Did the ending know it was coming? Was the ending surprised? What did the ending want for you? What happened after the ending? Write the questions down. Let the questions bring something new to this moment. Perhaps answer some of the questions. Perhaps just make a list of questions.

~

Where World Peace Begins

Invitation to Read

In "Anything, Everything" by Laura Grace Weldon (48), a playful grocery store conversation becomes a chance to discuss what the poet most wishes to find—not items such as peanut butter or rutabagas, but answers for how to find a resolution for war and an end to human suffering. It's a poem that straddles real life and the world of the imagination. How do we begin to take on challenges, such as living up to "our planet's highest possibilities"? Weldon ends the poem by pointing us toward spaciousness and imagination as a possible "starting place."

Invitation to Write

Why not follow Weldon's invitation for finding a starting place? Take a deep breath. Imagine what could happen in the next moment and the next and the next that would lead you and/or the planet toward living into the "highest possibility." Write into those imaginary steps.

or

Write about an imaginary grocery store in which you could find on the shelves the answers to everything the world needs to become a just, safe, loving, supportive, healthy, honest, honoring and *insert here every adjective you dream of* place. Tell us all about that store. Who shops there? Who doesn't? Who do you wish would shop there? What do things cost? Who owns the store? What happens when you take these "answers" off the shelves?

∾

OTHER POEMS THAT SPEAK TO STARTING PLACES:

"August Morning," Albert Garcia, 35.
"Chorus" from *The Cure At Troy*, Seamus Heaney, 106.
"Stages," Hermann Hesse, 176.
"You Are a Poem with Feet," Phyllis Cole-Dai, 178.

HOW TO MEET A DAY

We have little choice about what happens in a day. We have much more choice in how we meet what happens in a day. Writing poems can help us see those choices. When we show up with a pen in our hands, we change our relationship to the world. We become narrators of our own lives—able to frame the story of the moment and who we are in it in fresh ways.

~

Pledge Yourself

Invitation to Read

What would it look like if we acted with as much honor and dignity as possible? And what's at stake if we don't? That's what Diane Ackerman considers in "School Prayer" (100). In the second and fourth stanzas, she writes what she hopes to do, how she hopes to do it, and where. And in the first and third stanzas, Ackerman makes these pledges "in the name of" things of value and beauty in the natural world, such as "the wayfaring moon" and "the crowning seasons." It's a strong statement of intent, a powerful visioning of the best self and why it matters.

Invitation to Write

Write your own pledge. What do you swear you will do to live honorably? What will your roles be? What will you not do? In what way will you carry yourself as you do these things? Perhaps call on the natural world to help strengthen you and inspire you to meet a day in your "best" way. Perhaps begin as Ackerman does. Write, "In the name of _____," and invoke things in the world you most wish to care for—clean water, honeybees, ripe mangoes, polar bears. Then follow this with an attempt to say how you most wish to meet a day, perhaps using Ackerman's words, "I swear I will _____." Perhaps follow this pattern several times. In this way, you go back and forth between the outer world as it is and your inner world the way you might wish it would be.

Um, nota bene: This is a prompt for an aspirational poem. You may not live up to it, but it doesn't hurt to envision it.

∽

Take a Page from the Playbook of Something You Admire

Invitation to Read

"Sometimes objects stun me," writes Naomi Shihab Nye. "I touch them carefully, saying, tell me what you know."[5] This honoring and curiosity drive the poem "How to Live Like a Water Lily" (69). Annette Langlois Grunseth seems to receive dictation directly from a water lily. Written in second person command form, the poem reads as advice for the poet, and perhaps for readers, too, in how to meet a day, from beginning to end, starting with awakening and ending with folding "softly back into yourself" as daylight leaves.

Invitation to Write

Think of something in the natural world you admire. Make a list of what it does and how. How does it meet adversity? How is it resilient? What does it do or how does it show up in a way that inspires you? Perhaps do some research and learn more about how this thing survives, how it thrives. Write a "how to" poem. Perhaps title your poem "How to Live Like a _____," filling in the blank with the object/being of your inquiry.

~

Say Hello

Invitation to Read

"Hello" has become one of the most important words in my vocabulary for being more mindful and more present. Whenever I notice a feeling or circumstance is here—be it welcome or unwelcome—I greet it. Hello, stuck. Hello, frustration. Hello, slow car in front of me. Hello, gratefulness. Hello, river otter. And in this way, I find myself entering the world as it is. It's such a healing practice.

"Hello, sun in my face," writes Mary Oliver in "Why I Wake Early" (27). I love returning to this poem for its simple willingness to meet the world, to say hello. The poem basically extols the sun, detailing what it does, then ends with the speaker's response to the sun and how it becomes a doorway through which one might meet the rest of the world.

Invitation to Write

Try this: Say hello to something you meet daily. It might be something you admire: The stars? Soap? A tree? It might be something you would rather avoid. Traffic? Your neighbor's noisy dog? After greeting it, write about how this thing works. What does it do? What does it "preach"? What does it teach you about how you might meet the rest of the world?

~

OTHER POEMS THAT SPEAK TO HOW TO MEET A DAY:

"Basking," Martha Postlethwaite, 34.
"A Voice that Calms," Daniel Ladinsky, 65.
"Death," Ron Starbuck, 133.

QUIETUDE

In "What Stillness" (68), Laura Davies Foley writes, "What sunlight does to water, stillness does to us." What *does* stillness do to us? How does silence inform us and transform the way we meet a moment? It strikes me as a sweet paradox each time we sit down to write about silence. Obviously, to write about silence is to disturb it. But there is something wonderful that happens in me when I write about silence and stillness—a calm that comes, a centering that finds me, as if to touch silence with words is to invite it into me in new ways.

Remember the Silence

Invitation to Read

"I wish I'd had the sense to stay quiet," writes David Romtvedt in "Sunday Morning Early" (66). The poem is a lushly descriptive retelling of a morning in which the speaker and his daughter are in kayaks on a lake, and he feels an overwhelming need to comment on the moment. How often does this happen? We speak into a sacred hush, and in so doing, we discover, as the speaker does in this poem, that our comment has diminished the moment. As much as this poem beautifully depicts the lake scene around the boats, it also goes into thoughtful detail about what is happening inside the speaker. It's a very quiet but no less thrilling sweetness when, at the end of the poem, the speaker chooses not to say something and meets the moment in silence. In this way the poem begins with an outer silence, but it ends with an inner silence.

Invitation to Write

Write a poem that remembers a moment with another person that was enhanced by silence. Write into your memories of that moment. Use as many senses as make sense. How was the silence another participant in this scene? How did you respond to it? How did it respond to you? What went unsaid in that moment? What does that moment have to teach you now?

or

Find a silent space, either with another person or alone. Write a poem that notices how silence informs this moment. What is not here? What is here? What doesn't need to be said? What most rises to be said? What is the texture of this silence? How does it hold you? How does it feel foreign? What does it remind you of? What would make you leave this silence? How would you re-enter it?

～

Love Note to Silence

Invitation to Read

Writing an epistolary poem—a poem that feels like a letter—can be an easy way to employ conversational, intimate language, and it often helps with writer's block because letter-writing format is so familiar. In "Love Note to Silence" (33), José A. Alcántara writes to silence as if it is a lover. The speaker outlines places they've gone together and things they've done. He apologizes. He honors. He suggests a future trip. Alcántara's epistolic approach is a creative, personal way to explore our relationship with silence.

Invitation to Write

Write a poem that is a letter to silence. It may be a love letter, like Alcántara's. It may be a formal complaint. Whatever feels most true in this moment, write that. You might choose to bring up times when you and silence have been willing partners or when you have resisted each other. You might ask silence questions. Will it answer? You might tell it how you feel. You might confess your indiscretions. You might beg it for help. Notice that you could write this same poem again and again, and it might be very different every time you write it.

or

Imagine silence writes a poem letter to you. What would it say? What would it not say?

～

OTHER POEMS THAT SPEAK TO QUIETUDE:

"Nuthatch," Kirsten Dierking, 32.
"August Morning," Albert Garcia, 35.
"What Stillness," Laura Davies Foley, 68.
"The Wild Geese," Wendell Berry, 157.
"Limitless," Danna Faulds, 172.

ACCEPTANCE

We live in a culture that wants to know—we chart, graph, test, outline, classify, name and judge. But what of all the messiness, mystery and unruly potential that breeds beneath our longing for certainty? Life slips through any structure or stricture we might try to impose. My spiritual teacher, Joi Sharp, often asks, "Can you say yes to the world as it is?" This is the essence of acceptance. Or, as Danusha Laméris writes in "Cherries" (49), can you "take whatever falls into your hand"?

∼

Meeting the Truth We'd Rather Not Meet

Invitation to Read

In "Sheltered in Place" (46), Richard Levine writes about a "you" facing many truths that most of us would rather not meet. The many layers to this poem are complex, and Levine treats them with understanding and tenderness, but they all seem to point to this:

Everything dies, no matter how careful we are, no matter what care we take, no matter how much we might wish it were otherwise.

Invitation to Write

Think of a time when someone helped you meet a truth you did not want to meet. Where were you? What was happening? How was it different from what you wished would be happening? What did they say, or not say? What did they do, or not do? How did you resist what they told you? How did their actions or words help you say yes to the world as it is? Or not? If you could go back in time, what would you say to yourself in that moment? How might you comfort yourself?

~

"Say Only, Thank You"

Invitation to Read

One path toward acceptance is gratefulness. Ross Gay explores this in "Thank You" (54). Confronted with the fact that "all you love will turn to dust," the speaker of the poem suggests we notice what is happening all around us in the present and "Say only, thank you." Such an elegant call toward presence— to notice the sanctity of the moment and inhabit it fully.

Invitation to Write

Could it be this simple? Can the words "thank you" and the spirit of gratefulness help transform our relationship with our own impermanence and the impermanence of all we love, taking us from resistance to acceptance?

Try it out. Be honest. Write into your fears about losing those you love or losing your own life and then notice what is happening in the world all around you at this moment. Let the writing of those specific details—what you hear and see and taste and feel and smell—lead you into the present. Is gratefulness available right now? If yes, write about that gratefulness. If no, then write about what it is like right now to meet your own mortality and the mortality of all you love. What is it like to not be thankful in this very honest moment?

$\sim$

OTHER POEMS THAT SPEAK TO ACCEPTANCE:

"Cherries," Danusha Laméris, 49.
"In the Third Month of the Pandemic, My Husband Goes Through His Sock Drawer," Holly J. Hughes, 36.

HOW WE CARE FOR EACH OTHER
(& OURSELVES)

"There are many reasons to treat each other with great tenderness," I write in "Watching My Friend Pretend Her Heart Isn't Breaking" (126). And there are so many ways to express this tenderness, this willingness to care for each other. There are so many ways to treat each other with sensitivity and humanity, to be generous in our assumptions and unstinting in our support of each other (whether we know each other or not).

～

How We Might Hold Each Other

Invitation to Read

As our lives rush by, how do we choose to be more open to loving each other? How do we support other people in need? In "Divorce" (37), José A. Alcántara compares a friend who has recently been through a painful time to a hummingbird that has hit a window and now "lies stunned on the stone patio." With exquisite sensitivity, the speaker of the poem cradles the bird in his hands, honoring the vulnerability, beauty and strength of the bird. With admiration, he forecasts its eventual healing. Alcántara's poem is powerful in part because he never breaks the metaphor. We only know through the title that there's more to this poem than a human and a hummingbird.

Invitation to Write

Think of someone you know who is going through a difficult time. Imagine, as Alcántara does, that they are an injured animal (or plant?) that you might care for. How would you treat them then? Describe any details about the animal/friend that you admire. How are they responding to the injury? What can you do to help? What must they do for themselves? What might it look like when they are healed? What feelings does it bring out in you?

~

Recalling the Hands That Healed Us

Invitation to Read

There is so much intimacy in the way Li-Young Lee remembers how his father pulled a splinter from his finger when he was a child in "The Gift" (44). He recalls the look on the father's face, the "two measures of tenderness" that were his father's hands. He remembers feeling as if he would die, and he also brings in some of the details he doesn't remember—a fabulous technique for helping to convey the tone of a moment. The poem carries forward into how the speaker in the poem now removes a splinter from his wife's hand with great care. In this way, the legacy of someone else's ability to love and to care is passed on through us.

Invitation to Write

Think of a moment in your life when you felt taken care of—when someone else treated you with great kindness. Bring in details of their hands, of your fears, of their voice, of the light in that moment. What do you not remember? How did you respond to their care? How does this moment from the past relate to you right now? What does it whisper to you? Perhaps this will be the whole poem—responding to the care you received. Or perhaps, as Lee does, you'll include another time in which you returned this kindness to another, passing on the care that you were given. How does that moment of your own caring affect you now?

∾

Treating Each Other Like Family

Invitation to Read

How do we get ahead in life? "It's who you know." But what if you don't know the "right" people for getting ahead? Examining the privilege of association and pledging help to another is at the heart of Mohja Kahf's "The Aunty Poem (Mi Privilege Es Tu Privilege)" (144). Written in second person as a promise or pledge, the poem is filled with specific details about how the speaker will honor and care for and support the "you" in the poem. "I will introduce you to whatever board members I know" comes soon after offering the use of an ironing board. It's a poem that is both playful and very serious about how we might give our support—financial, emotional, professional and foundational—to someone else who needs it. The poem also suggests ways the relationship will be reciprocal.

Invitation to Write

How far would you go to help someone else? What likely and unlikely resources do you have to offer? What do they need that you can give? Be very honest. Be very specific. Offer only what you can without being resentful. What would you wish for in return? What do you not need in return?

or

Think of a time when someone of no relation took you in as a treasured family member. Write them a poem that is a thank you letter. Use specific details about how they supported you. What did their actions mean to you then? What do they mean to you now? How do you imagine that experience might affect your future? How does it change the way you treat other people?

or

Think of a time when you needed help and didn't receive it. How has that experience shaped the way you are meeting this moment? What would you tell that younger version of yourself now? What do you think that younger version might say to the present you?

What Would the Jacket Say?

Invitation to Read

Sometimes a single strong image can tell us so much about how to take care of each other. This is the case with the simple scene that Naomi Shihab Nye shares in "Shoulders" (43). The speaker sees a man carrying a sleeping child on his shoulder across traffic in the rain. With careful attention to detail, Shihab Nye shares with us about the weather, the street, the sound of the boy's breath. She also tells us what isn't there: "Nowhere does his jacket say FRAGILE, HANDLE WITH CARE." The poem ends by asking us to consider what this scenario has to teach us about how we treat other people. There's an urgency in the poem as it ends with an imperative. Though it won't be easy, when it comes to taking care of each other, "we must."

Invitation to Write

This poem suggests a simple form: Show us a scene, then tell us why it matters. Try it. Think of a time when you saw a colleague or family member or stranger caring for someone else's life as if it were the most precious possession. Describe the scene in detail. Then let us know what this small moment has to say to the big world. You don't have to be wise—you could ask a question instead of delivering a truth. But wonder about it—how might one small act of caring inform the balance of what it means to be human?

or

What words can you imagine would be written on another person's jacket? If humans came with instructions on how they need to be touched and held and treated, what would the instructions say? Write a poem that creates a new line of clothing. Or a closet full of clothes you can wear that tell the world how you would like to be treated. Or make a new wardrobe for someone you care for that instructs the rest of the world how to take care of them.

or

Think of a time when someone "carried" you. Write about what it felt like to know that someone had you, that you were safe with them, so safe that you could give them your full weight. Write that person a poem, basically a thank you letter, describing what that moment meant to you then and what it means now as you continue to move forward.

~

OTHER POEMS THAT SPEAK TO HOW WE CARE FOR EACH OTHER (AND OURSELVES):

"The Healing Time," Pesha Joyce Gertler, 38.
"People Who Take Care," Nancy Henry, 59.
"At the Cancer Clinic," Ted Kooser, 60.
"Small Kindnesses," Danusha Laméris, 142.
"Love and Fear in a Pandemic," Christine Stewart-Nuñez, 162.
"when we get through this," Maya Stein, 165.

FEELING INTO COMPASSION

One of my favorite definitions of compassion comes from "Phase One" (39) by Dilruba Ahmed. Compassion is when you "find a way to become the love that you want in this world." It is less, perhaps, about "I am going to help you" and more about acting on behalf of our shared humanity. As Ram Dass said in an interview with Raghu Markus, "it's like one hand pulling the other hand out of the fire. It's all part of the same body. That's true compassion."[6]

How can writing help us explore how it is to reach into the fire to save our other hand?

≈

Heroes of the Heart

Invitation to Read

In Gloria Heffernan's poem "You Just Never Know" (120), she invites us to look past our biases about who might be wise in the ways of compassion. The speaker begins by humanizing her mother, explaining the religious and spiritual practices she *didn't* engage in, then wryly depicting the mother's "mudra" as holding a cigarette and a coffee cup. With this basis, she then hails how her mother has become a guiding grace in her life with her "mantra" of "You just never know." The speaker shows us specific instances in daily life where she draws on her mother's example "to create more space for compassion." In fact, the poem itself has a satisfying meta quality in celebrating its unlikely heart hero, underscoring the wisdom of *you just never know.*

Invitation to Write

Who inspires you to be more compassionate? Is it something they say? Something they do? A specific instance you can recall? Or a pattern of compassion you've watched for years? Write a poem that portrays this person and honors their capacity for compassion. Be specific. You may want to do what Heffernan does and paint them as an unlikely hero. You may want to include instances from your own life and show how their example has shaped who you are now.

How Compassion Guides Us

Invitation to Read

It can be so difficult to be present with someone who is suffering. In "Compassion" (122), James Crews takes us into the hospital room where the speaker is sitting with his dying father for the last time. "Compassion sat quietly beside me," Crews writes, personifying compassion. I think it's interesting that the poem is written in hindsight, as if, in the moment, the speaker was unaware of just how present compassion was. But in recalling the time in the hospital room, the speaker is now clear how compassion helped guide his actions and interactions with his father.

Compassion helped the speaker be present to what was being asked of him. By using specific details about a bottle of Coke, unwrapping a straw, the quality of his own voice, and the way he held his father's hands, Crews lets us not only see the scene but also smell the perfume of presence. He invites us into that room as well, invites us to notice what a friend and guide compassion can be.

Invitation to Write

Think of a time when you were with someone who was struggling—a time when, perhaps you, too, were struggling to know how to be with them. Write into that moment. Perhaps even imagine you are watching the movie of this scene. Where does the camera focus—in close or wide lens? What details does it pick up? Now consider what was happening inside of you? What do you know now about that moment that you didn't know then? How can you see that compassion was present? What details help you see that you were led by compassion?

Or, perhaps, you notice compassion was *not* present. How might that moment have unfolded differently if you had been guided by compassion? Perhaps wonder about it in your poem. Are you able to be compassionate now with yourself about your actions and interactions in that moment?

OTHER POEMS THAT SPEAK TO FEELING INTO COMPASSION:

"Phase One," Dilruba Ahmed, 39.
"Shoulders," Naomi Shihab Nye, 43.

"Slowing Down," Ruby R. Wilson, 47.
"Watching My Friend Pretend Her Heart Isn't Breaking,"
    Rosemerry Wahtola Trommer, 126.

HOW WE MIGHT COME TOGETHER

In the epigraph to *Poetry of Presence II*, Ada Limón asks, "What is it to go to a *We* from an *I*?" Our survival as a species depends on the answer to this question. In Rumi's poem, "Elephant in the Dark" (173), translated by Coleman Barks and John Moyne, it's suggested that "if each of us held a candle" at the edge of the darkness and "went in together" we would have a much clearer vision of what it is to be alive in this world.

What is our work as poets to "hold a candle"? Here's a challenge —to stand unflinchingly in the messy center and write what it looks like when we come together.

~

Together in the Big Disaster

Invitation to Read

In "Here Together" (70), W. S. Merwin compares surviving a day to surviving being "swept away" by a swift body of water with a strong current. The speaker and the "you" in the poem survive by clinging to each other. There is something about meeting the dangerous conditions together that keeps the people in the poem alive.

For many of us who have been through difficult times, we know the truth of this poem—how in the "blur" of tough moments, it is often our connection to other people that allows us to stay present. That doesn't mean we escape the mess; it just means we are able to meet it and metaphorically keep our heads above water.

What strikes me about Merwin's poem is that he doesn't seem to see an end in sight. The end of the poem with its unanswered questions seems to suggest the struggle will go on and on, perhaps forever—and yet, there is the comfort of clinging to each other, and meeting the difficulty together.

Another example of a disaster metaphor being used this way is toward the end of Alison Luterman's poem "A few days after my first vaccine," (164). Here, Luterman likens the ways we survive the pandemic to finding a "raft to grab onto in the wake of a shipwreck."

Another literal example of this can be found in "House of Mercury" (93), in which Fady Joudah writes about a storm that caused considerable damage to the trees in a family's yard and how the neighbors—a culturally diverse group—came to help. The poem shares both the destruction and the generosity of spirit that it elicited. By the end of the poem, there is a reframing of the disaster—how now the mother's "morning glories will get the light they deserve." It's a powerful movement from the destruction in line one to the promise of beauty in the last line—and in this way, the poem literally moves us from one framework to another.

Invitation to Write

Think of a natural disaster—an earthquake, a tsunami, a hurricane, a mudslide, a flash flood. Or perhaps a human disaster—a house fire, a shipwreck, a plane crash. Make a list of as many words as you can think of that relate to this disaster. You can draw on these for the poem.

Now think of a person whom you are helping, or who is helping you, as you get through a difficult time, past or present. Write about this time as if it is the two of you facing this natural or human disaster together—use it as a metaphor for what is happening in real life. How do you work together? What happens with your bodies? What feelings do you have about the situation? About the other person? What does this metaphor have to teach you about how you are responding to a challenge? Perhaps steal Merwin's first line (and give credit by italicizing the borrowed line and adding an attribution to the Merwin and his poem's title beneath your title): "These days I can see us _____."

or

If you feel as if you *do not* have someone helping you meet a challenging time, then write about what it is like to meet the disaster on your own. Maybe write about what it would be like to have a partner in this time. If the poem is aspirational, you can insert the words "I wish" to make it true. For instance, "These days, I wish I could see us _____."

⁓

Make Up a Game

Invitation to Read

There's a sweet humor to "Passing the Orange" (50), in which Leo Dangel writes about a teacher who got all the parents in a classroom to stand in two lines, one line of men, one line of women. Their task is to pass an orange down the line holding the orange only with their chins. Dangel depicts the dads as unlikely candidates for playing this game with any success—in fact, they seem unlikely candidates to play this game at all.

How often do we think we can predict what someone else will or won't do? How often do we predict people won't work well together when they are uncomfortable? What a gift to ourselves when we see we are proven wrong in our assumptions. Though the dads in the poem complain, they succeed. The triumph in that classroom sings through the page as these men practice working together as a team in a rather goofy, even compromising, circumstance.

Invitation to Write

Think of people who you believe will not get along. They could be fictional characters or real, historical or present day, or a mix of both. Write a poem in which you have your characters play a game together that relies on them being a team. Write about how they struggle. What do you imagine they are feeling? What must they set aside to be able to participate? How do they accomplish that? How do they show up in the moment to work with an unlikely teammate? It's up to you if they succeed in their task in the end. What do you think they learn? What did you learn from stepping into their shoes?

~

OTHER POEMS THAT SPEAK TO HOW WE MIGHT COME TOGETHER:

"Fused," Gloria Heffernan, 64.
"Patriotism," Elle Schoenfeld, 136.
"U Pick," Barbara Crooker, 139.
"Elephant in the Dark," Rumi, translated by Coleman Barks and
     John Moyne, 173.

CONNECTING WITH THE
NATURAL WORLD

"Natural spaces sharpen our senses, help us tune in, and make us more aware of being alive," write the editors in the introduction to *Poetry of Presence II*. Nature is, as they say, "an effective mindfulness teacher." Though this collection mostly focuses on finding mindfulness in human interaction, there are still poems here that invite us to explore our connection to the more than human world.

Often, when I do not know what to write about, I will go for a walk outside, or just sit outside and let my senses open. What do I hear? What do I smell? What do I see? What do I not see? Eventually I let my attention rest on something, anything. It ever amazes me how *everything* can be a partner and guide in our understanding of what it is to be alive. I often ask, though I don't always hear or intuit an answer, "What do you have to teach me?" Sometimes just sitting with that question is everything.

∾

Pledging Allegiance to the Earth

Invitation to Read

Ask almost any gardener: there is something deeply healing and wholesome about digging in the dirt, and in "Patriotism" (136), Ellie Schoenfeld not only finds herself kneeling in the dirt, but ends up pledging allegiance to this land, to "all the dirt of the world." Schoenfeld writes about who her "compatriots" are and how they interact with no judgment, no malice. The poem invokes a powerful wish for a country—that it be a place where we feel accepted and where our "true substance" is *known*. The poem also serves as a reminder of how beneficial it can be to our being to work with the soil, to get dirt under our fingernails, to remember where our bodies have come from and where they are going.

Invitation to Write

To pledge allegiance is to pledge loyalty and commitment to something larger than ourselves. If you were to write your own pledge of allegiance to the earth or to the natural world, what would it be? What is it about the earth that would make you want to pledge yourself to it? Who are your compatriots? What is your common goal? Your common ground? What does this pledge have to teach you about your relationship with the world?

"Earth's Intelligence"

Invitation to Read

What would it look like, as Rainer Maria Rilke writes, "if we surrendered to earth's intelligence"? In his poem "How surely gravity's law" (171), translated by Anita Barrow and Joanna Macy, Rilke explores one of the essential forces of this world—gravity—and uses it to look at human resistance. How difficult it can be for us to "surrender"! And yet, as Rilke suggests, if we do, we might "rise up rooted, like trees." *If* is such a powerful word for inviting our imaginations—for invoking possibility and openness.

Invitation to Write

Write a poem that observes something that occurs in the natural world. Rilke is examining a force (gravity), but you could examine how honey is made, or how antelope surround the young and hurt when sensing attack, or how a river shapes a landscape. Explore this phenomenon. Perhaps research it. Then wonder how this "earth intelligence" might change your life if you could follow it. What does it have to teach you? What do you wonder about how it works? How do you resist such intelligence? Why do you resist it? Perhaps use a line like Rilke's to prompt yourself into discovery: "This is what the things can teach us."

~

OTHER POEMS THAT SPEAK TO CONNECTING WITH THE NATURAL WORLD:

"The One and Only Day," Tom Hennen, 26.
"Can You Hear It?" Paula Lepp, 31.
"Nuthatch," Kirsten Dierking, 32.
"How to Live Like a Water Lily," Annette Langlois Grunseth, 69.
"On the Day After You Left This World," Heather Swan, 132.
"Give Me This," Ada Limón, 138.
"The Wild Geese," Wendell Berry, 157.
"Belonging," Rosemerry Wahtola Trommer, 167.

WHAT REALLY MATTERS

Perhaps you have had moments when you look around and say to yourself, "What are you *doing*? Is *this* where you want to put your attention and time?" Sometimes this kind of radical self-inquiry happens after trauma. Sometimes it happens in the middle of an unremarkable Tuesday. It feels like a gift when it happens—this sudden ability to see what is essential and what is dross.

Again, I find myself returning to the work of poetry—how it helps us ask the question "What does it mean to be alive?" Apparently one answer is sometimes we lose track of what's important. And another answer is, sometimes we find our way *back* to what's important. For me, mindfulness poems, with their insistence on meeting the moment and returning to "what is true," are helpful guides that help us dig through the detritus to get to the heart of our lives.

∾

Write Your Dream Lesson

Invitation to Read

Play is one of the most powerful tools we have for dancing with difficult truths. Brad Aaron Modlin shows us how much fun we can have as we get curious about what really matters. In "What You Missed That Day You Were Absent from Fourth Grade" (51), Modlin shares the curriculum for a single school day—the one none of us ever had—in which all of life's greatest questions are answered, or at least are met.

Part of the joy in this poem is how it embraces both the sacred and profane at the same time. The teacher instructs on "how to find meaning in pumping gas" and "how to chant the Psalms during cigarette breaks." Each line is a new pleasure—I find myself thinking, "Yes, I want to learn that!" And the creative framework that Modlin has chosen (a school day) allows something that could also be very serious to become a source of creative delight.

Invitation to Write

Imagine that there was a day in school that you missed that would have taught you everything you now wish you had learned at a younger age. Could be any grade. Could be one teacher or many. What skills do you wish you had been taught to make you a better human? Make a list, as Modlin does. Perhaps use two-line stanzas, as in Modlin's poem, which allows for a lot of spaciousness. See how classroom imagery, such as chalkboards or whiteboards or desks or rulers or quizzes, might lead you into surprising places.

or

Knowing what you know now, what advice would you give your fourth-grade self about how to best meet the path that your life has taken?

~

Sing What Is Now

Invitation to Read

Holly Wren Spaulding's poem "At the New Year" (56) shows us how a very small moment (and a very small poem) can have a very large impact. There are no big words, no grandiose ideas, no shocking revelations in this brief poem, yet it does a great job of helping us notice what matters. Spaulding goes back and forth between showing and telling—showing us details around her, such as "bean soup in a white bowl," and telling us her inner response to seeing these things in this one moment. The poem doesn't reach beyond the moment, it simply sings of what is now. It's such a simple invitation—and it touches something deep.

Invitation to Write

In this very moment, look around. What gives you pleasure? What surprises you with its "thisness," as Gerard Manley Hopkins would say? What do you notice inside you this moment about your response (or lack of response) to these things? If you look around and find that *nothing* is giving you pleasure, that might be a very interesting poem to write, too—one that helps you really be curious about what matters.

~

OTHER POEMS THAT SPEAK TO WHAT REALLY MATTERS:

"Ten Thousand Flowers in Spring," Wu-Men, translated
    by Stephen Mitchell, 55.
"Love and Fear in a Pandemic," Christine Stewart-Nuñez, 162.

GROWING INTO OURSELVES

We are ever-growing, ever-evolving versions of ourselves, and poetry can be such a powerful way to notice what changes are happening, what changes have already happened, and where might we go from here.

~

The Drive to Bloom

Invitation to Read

Sometimes, in the direst circumstances, we find it in us to bloom. Linda Hogan describes this phenomenon in "Geraniums" (135). She describes a situation of neglect and how, despite lack of care, as if lit from within, the abandoned geraniums still manage to flower. What begins as an observation becomes an exhortation. The second half of the poem speaks directly to a "you" in difficult circumstances. "You can't bloom that way," Hogan writes, and the poem instills an urgency in escaping those circumstances so that blooming becomes possible.

How often do we cut ourselves off from our own growth by placing ourselves (and our thoughts) in unnourishing environments?

Invitation to Write

Write a poem in which you are a flower. Are you about to bloom? Past bloom? Blooming even now? What kind of soil are you in? Is it soil that nurtures you? Or are you blooming only because you are so determined to bloom, despite circumstances? What do you lack? What do you have in abundance? Are there other flowers or other beings growing around you? What does this metaphor teach you about your own growth in this moment?

~

Learn from the Best Growers on the Planet

Invitation to Read

In "Redwood Dharma" (170), Laura Grace Weldon writes of the redwood trees and shares facts about how they grow. It's a poem that relies almost completely on "show"—giving us the specific details of longevity, strength and support. It's only in the last two lines that Weldon "tells" us the metaphor—inviting us to revisit the facts of the redwood vis-à-vis our own lives.

Invitation to Write

Choose any animal, plant or fungus and research how it survives. How does it grow? How does it interact with other members of its species? Notice in your research when you get excited about a certain fact. Write a poem of facts, and then, like Weldon, suggest how your subject might have something essential to teach you as you work to survive.

or

Perhaps you want to show how humans might *not* want to take a cue from the species you're researching.

～

OTHER POEMS THAT SPEAK TO GROWING INTO OURSELVES:

"What You Missed That Day You Were Absent from Fourth
    Grade," Brad Aaron Modlin, 51.
"Addition," Carrie Newcomer, 52.
"Allow," Danna Faulds, 53.

MEETING MORTALITY

I remember hearing an interview with Charles Wright on *Poets in Person* in which he said all poems are about death. I was in my early twenties then, and I completely disagreed. Three decades later, I think he's spot on. A poem is a chance to explore what it is to be alive, and that exploration is made more poignant by the certainty that we, and everyone we love, will die.

Some poems circle this truth, but others directly engage with mortality. Far from morbid, these poems are often life-affirming invitations to be humble, to be clear in our purpose, to be generous in how we treat other people. They can inspire us to consider our priorities and grow into our full potential in the time we've been given. They invite us to live well and to die well.

~

What If You Knew

Invitation to Read

Ellen Bass's poem "If You Knew" (114) begins with a strong question: "What if you knew you'd be the last to touch someone?" Bass uses daily interactions, a personal story, and a series of unanswered questions to explore the answer.

Moving through life with this question might change how we treat other people, if only in our thoughts. How differently might we feel about the driver who speeds past us, the woman behind the cash register, the man muttering to himself in the park?

This is an example of how poems are powerful frames that can change our vision, our choices, our words. A poem can act like a lens that allows us to see a familiar situation with new eyes.

Invitation to Write

Think about your recent past. What interactions did you have with someone you didn't know well? If you knew they would die after you saw them, how might you have treated them or thought of them differently? The entire poem might be made of questions about alternate ways that interaction might have played out.

or

Sit for a while with this thought: You could die at any moment. How does thinking about your own mortality change the way you want to interact with other people as you move forward from this moment? Another idea: Look to the past and choose a specific moment you would like to redo. What do you know now that you didn't know then?

∿

Saying Goodbye

Invitation to Read

When we are with the dying in their last moments, how do we show up? What do we say? What do we notice? Dylan Thomas famously wrote to his father, "Do not go gentle into that good night." But Linda Pastan, meeting her own father's death, advises the opposite in her poem "Go Gentle" (129). She shares details of the final days, shares a memory from when her father gave her advice and shares what she longs to say, but she doesn't tell us if she said the words or not. She also notices what is happening in the outside world as her father is nearing his final breath. It's a tender and quiet poem, a small poem that finds the balancing point of the past and present, life and death, holding on and letting go.

Invitation to Write

If you have been with someone in their final days, consider writing a poem that speaks about that time. What did you say? What did you not say? What did they say or not say? What was present? How did the season affect the mood? How would you meet that moment differently now if you could? Or would you do it the same?

or

Imagine your death. How do you think you would like other people to treat you when you are dying? What conversations would you most wish to have? What do you hope would remain unsaid? Who do you hope would be there? Perhaps start with the line, "And if I die in springtime _____."

∽

Memento Mori

Invitation to Read

Knowing you will die, and bringing this fact to mind, how might you live your life differently today? The Stoic philosophers would say *Memento mori*, "Remember your death." And that is exactly the opportunity we are given in "Death" by Ron Starbuck (133). Starbuck asks many questions that bid us think about what it will be like when we die (and after), and then he offers a suggestion for how we might meet other people while we are still alive.

Invitation to Write

Make a list of questions you have about your own death. You do not need to answer them, (nor can you, really). Make a poem out of this list, or perhaps delve into one question that really interests you.

or

If you would rather *not* write a poem about mortality, perhaps start with this line: "I don't want to remember that I will die," and see where that leads you.

OTHER POEMS THAT SPEAK TO MEETING MORTALITY:

"Sheltered in Place," Richard Levine, 46.
"Thank You," Ross Gay, 54.
"Fused," Gloria Heffernan, 64.
"Sunday Morning Early," David Romtvedt, 66.
"The Pedicure," Annette Langlois Grunseth, 113.

BEING PRESENT WITH A LOVED ONE'S ABSENCE

It's one thing to imagine how we might meet a death, it's quite another to meet death after it has happened. How do we show up in these moments of great loss? How do we support other people who are going through grief?

Reading poems can help us see how other individuals have met these moments. And when we are writing a poem, we can trust that no matter what we are feeling, the blank page will meet us exactly there. It won't ask us to be brave or wise or generous. We can simply show up and write what is true.

~

What Does Your Loved One Say?

Invitation to Read

Sometimes after a loved one has died, we hold on to something of theirs—a piece of clothing, a bit of jewelry, a pen, or, as in "Cold Solace" by Anna Belle Kaufman (130), some food that they made, saved in the freezer. I love how intentional the speaker in the poem is, taking the cake out, slicing it, admiring it.

When things are linked to our dead beloveds, they can take on great importance. In this poem, I'm aware of how much reverence there is for this cake made by a deceased mother. The reverence, of course, is for the mother herself. I welcome the conceit that the mother speaks through the cake—that the poet interprets what wisdom and insight the "amber squares" might have to offer. It implies a deep knowing of the person who is gone—hearing their voice come through the object, through the veil of death, to offer us some counsel on what it is to be alive.

Invitation to Write

If you have an object that belonged to a person you love who has died, write about that object. What is it like? Describe it in detail. What was your loved one's relationship to it? What do you want to remember about your loved one? If speaking to you through this object, what would they say? What might they tell you about how to meet this very moment?

≈

What Is Really Here?

Invitation to Read

There can be, after a death, a period of almost astonishing receptivity, as if our brokenness allows for an unprecedented openness. Such openness is at the heart of Heather Swan's poem "On the Day After You Left This World" (132). Shortly after a death, the speaker goes out into the world believing she is seeking one thing. What she finds is something very different.

What strikes me about this poem is the power in acknowledging the gap between our expectations and reality. The speaker seems to surrender to *the world that is* instead of continuing to seek *the world she thought she would find.* Ultimately, it is a poem of connection—how in the face of loss, the speaker in the poem comes to feel very intimately connected, unified, even, with the world and its sounds, light, temperature, elements, and animals. Part of how Swan establishes this unification is through subtle alliteration—literally joining disparate items by giving them a similarity of sound. For instance, one line includes "cranes, crickets, cattails" and the next line gives us the "broken body breathing." The unifying effect the sounds have on the ear helps assist the unifying effect the poem has on the heart.

Invitation to Write

In this moment, think of someone who has died. Imagine how you might wish to have met their loss. What feelings do you wish you might have had? What feelings would you rather not have had? How did the room or the world itself rise to meet you (or not) when you heard that your dear one died?

Now write about what is actually happening. In this moment, thinking of your dear one's death, what feelings do you have? What feelings do you not have? How does the room or the world meet you —what sounds, what temperature, what light, what other presences are here? How do you respond to them?

$\sim$

OTHER POEMS THAT SPEAK TO BEING PRESENT WITH ABSENCE:

"Watching My Friend Pretend Her Heart Isn't Breaking,"
    Rosemerry Wahtola Trommer, 126.
"While the World Burned On," Heather Swan, 127.

FINDING PURPOSE IN OUR WORK
IN THE WORLD

Sometimes a poem will come right out and tell us what it is we are here to do. I'll never forget the first time I read Mary Oliver's words, "My work is loving the world."[7] How my heart leapt up! And in *Poetry of Presence II*, there are many poems that astonish me with their ability to say so clearly what it is we are here to do.

But how do we arrive at such clarity? Writing can help. What happens if you make a short mad lib by filling in this sentence, "My work is _____."

In a single moment there might be many, many, many true ways to fill in that sentence. What is your work right now? Perhaps write a whole list. Then, perhaps, choose one purpose from your list that has juice in it and explore it.

∾

My Sole Purpose

Invitation to Read

Every moment asks something of us—invites us to meet it in a certain way. In "Basking" (34), Martha Postlethwaite describes the light in the room and how it invites her to show up. It's a simple poem with a simple invitation that seems to have enormous implications—can we do what is asked of us in the moment? Can we discern in any given moment what our sole purpose is?

Invitation to Write

Describe where you are right now. What is around you? What is the light like? Who else is with you? What does this very moment ask of you? Perhaps use these words: "My sole purpose is to _____." Or, perhaps allow wonder to lead you into an exploration with this phrase, "Is my sole purpose to _____?"

∽

The Workers Who Inspire Us

Invitation to Read

In "To Be of Use" (58), Marge Piercy writes about the people who give themselves over completely to their work. In the first two stanzas, the poet honors how completely suited these workers are to their environments—"They seem to become natives of that element." Piercy compares the workers to seals in the sea and then to water buffalo "who strain in the mud" to get the work done. Piercy also names workers who are not inspiring, then holds them up against those who labor, who are common, who are hardworking in daily ways. The poem uses many short, Germanic words (*botched, mud, dust, task, muck),* and in this way it honors a more basic, less flowery way of being in the world, appealing to a human need to be useful.

Invitation to Write

What workers do you admire? What do you admire about them? Describe them in their working environment. How do they move? What do they do? What do they not do? What does their work have to teach you about your work in the world? If you need a starting place, consider using Piercy's line, "I love the people who _____."

~

Engaging with Opposition

Invitation to Read

What is our work as bridgebuilders? In "Holding the Light" by Stuart Kestenbaum (158), the speaker in the poem points out many opposites: earth/sky, glitter/gutter, day/night, self/world. What is a person to do when confronted with so much opposition?

Kestenbaum writes, "In our imperfect world we are meant to . . . ." The answer given in the poem is both abstract and concrete. It feels both practical and metaphorical. I love how the poem itself does what it is asking its reader to do—it stitches together oppositions and makes something new of them, something radiant, "a blessing."

Note that the poem, written in second person, offers instructions. Also, note that it ends with encouragement. There are many ways to end a poem "right." How does this ending suit the poem?

~

OTHER POEMS THAT SPEAK TO FINDING PURPOSE IN OUR WORK IN THE WORLD:

"Instructions to the Worker Bee," Lucy Adkins, 57.
"People Who Take Care," Nancy Henry, 59.
"Work Was His Religion," Marjorie Saiser, 112.

FINDING BEAUTY & FULLNESS
AMIDST HEARTBREAK

One of the greatest mysteries of being alive is that the world is simultaneously full of heartache and sorrow, beauty and joy. How do we reconcile this in our own being? My beloved poetry friend Jack Mueller used to growl, "Power to the paradox." And there it is.

This, to me, is the real work of a poem: to somehow allow the writer and reader to enter two worlds at once, not trying to deny one world or the other, but honoring how there is always a full spectrum of emotional possibility.

∾

Is It a Beautiful Day?

Invitation to Read

How often do we close ourselves off to the beauty around us? How often do we tune out the voices around us? In "Overheard" (141), Ross Gay writes about an interaction in which he must hear the phrase "It's a beautiful day" multiple times before he acknowledges the speaker, the message, and the truth of the message. At the heart of the poem is a single beautiful image—a sunrise in a specific place in a specific time. Surrounding that image is a powerful story—how the self might unfold and bloom, opening to the surrounding beauty, if only we pay attention and let the world in.

Speaking of paradox, I admire how Gay includes what is not going right in the world by referring to what wasn't said. In this way, what is difficult is both here and not here at the same time. Gay's acknowledgement of how difficult life can be allows the beauty at the center of the poem to truly shine.

Invitation to Write

Imagine that someone is right now saying to you, "It's a beautiful day." Notice any part of you that wants to ignore or to argue with this declaration. Write about that resistance.

Now, look around you for one bit of evidence that it is true, *It's a beautiful day*. Write about this proof—describe it in detail. Perhaps you wish to also write about all the evidence to the contrary. Why is it not a beautiful day? Let these two declarations exist in the same poem. Notice that how you choose to end the poem makes a big difference in the overall tenor.

or

Write about what is keeping you from noticing beauty in the world in this moment. What voices or images or thoughts are you not allowing in?

∽

Carry Something Beautiful in Your Heart

Invitation to Read

Years ago I first read these words attributed to French mathematician Blaise Pascal, "In difficult times, carry something beautiful in your heart." In this one sentence, we are offered a way to move through the world no matter how challenging it is. Carry something beautiful in your heart. It sounds overly simple, and yet I have found it is profoundly effective. It does not in any way negate or deny the existence of cruelty, destruction, violence, inequality and loss. However, it keeps me from believing that these difficult circumstances are all there is.

When I wrote "Why I Smile at Strangers" (143), I was very consciously selecting things to keep in my heart—creating a small inventory of beauty to carry with me. It's just a list, really. But then, it seems to me, the invitation is not only to carry the beauty in our hearts, but to share it.

Invitation to Write

Make a list of beautiful things you can carry with you in your heart. Perhaps you are also aware of why it is so necessary in this moment to have such an inventory. Write about that, too. What is happening right now that discourages you? What do you notice about carrying something beautiful in your heart? How does it change the way you meet the difficult world? Or does it not change anything? How might you share this beauty? If you do share it, what effect do you notice the sharing has?

❧

OTHER POEMS THAT SPEAK TO FINDING BEAUTY AND FULLNESS:

"I Tell You," Susan Glassmeyer, 61.
"An Apple Tree Was Concerned," Daniel Ladinsky, 169.

HOW GRATEFULNESS CHANGES THE WORLD

There is incredible power in saying thank you—even if we are unsure about who or what we are saying thank you to. As Benedictine monk Brother David Steindl-Rast writes, "It is not happiness that makes us grateful. It is gratefulness that makes us happy."[8]

We could say there are three kinds of gratefulness poems:

1. Those that list many things to be grateful for
2. Those that explore gratefulness for a specific moment
3. Those that explore gratefulness for a specific thing (or collection of things)

Notice, as you write such poems, what effect(s) the writing has on your body.

∾

Thankful for Now

Invitation to Read

There are moments when we are stunned by the gift of being alive. Sometimes in these moments, as in "Thankful for Now" by Todd Davis (67), all our senses seem to go on high alert and open to let all the details of the moment in. I appreciate how Davis's poem has an almost cinematic quality because of the precise details—which bugs are present, which birds, what temperature, what terrain, what physical pose, what light, what sounds, what movement. It's like watching a very short film. The tension in the poem comes from knowing this beauty is ephemeral—not only the beauty itself, but the speaker's ability to even be in the moment. It's only a single line of the poem, but an essential one, that nods to how the speaker will not always have enough strength to follow his sons, walking the river home after a day of fishing. That touchpoint of aging and mortality is what grounds the gratefulness.

Invitation to Write

Think of a recent moment when you were completely aware of how grateful you were to be alive. Write into that moment. Recreate it through specific sensory details on the page. What was it about that moment that enlivened you? Consider including a line or two that nods to your own mortality. Notice the effect that has on the poem. Notice the effect it has on you.

❧

Bringing Gratefulness in Through the Senses

Invitation to Read

What sense do you rely on the most for gathering information about the world? In "Blessing for Sound" (175), David Whyte explores all the ways sound invites a person into the moment, into a life. The poet invokes specific sounds, "gull cries" or "a ship's horn," but he also explores how all sound comes together in one great soundtrack, and importantly, the poem explores how sound connects us to a "you"—perhaps a creator or God or the universe or the Beloved or life itself. I personally love how the poem both begins and ends in a pre-waking state, a state below consciousness in which we are somehow still receptive.

Invitation to Write

Choose a physical sense through which to explore gratefulness. Maybe choose one you seem to rely on the least. Write a poem that is a thank you letter to God or the creator or life itself for the ability to access the world through this sense. You might begin, as Whyte does, with "I thank you for _____." This poem can be a simple list. Perhaps imagine what life would be like without this sense. What would be missing? When is this sense most alert? How does it bring you into a closer relationship with the world?

❧

OTHER POEMS THAT SPEAK TO GRATEFULNESS:

"February 14," Kim Addonizio, 63.
"Fused," Gloria Heffernan, 64.
"Blessing for the Light," David Whyte, 159.

LEARNING MORE ABOUT GENEROSITY

One of my favorite definitions of generosity is from the University of Notre Dame's "Science of Generosity" website, which suggests that generosity "involves both attitude and action—entailing as a virtue both an inclination or predilection to give liberally and an actual practice of giving liberally." They propose that generosity is not inherent—it's a *learned* character trait. And one of the best ways, I think, to learn generosity is to study it and be wildly curious about it in other people. That's one of the gifts of reading these poems from *Poetry of Presence II.*

∾

How Generosity Changes a Moment

Invitation to Read

An act of generosity can have enormous power to move us—to change our state of mind from unease to peace. Consider the poem "Nor'easter" (74), in which James Crews wakes up with a feeling of dread, but when his father-in-law kindly plows out his drive after a sudden snowstorm, the poet finds himself on a path toward hope. The poem describes a single unselfish act, but it also nods to an ongoing generosity that seems to change not only the tenor of the day but the poet himself. The literal act of creating passage becomes a metaphor for moving forward.

Invitation to Write

Who has been generous to you with their actions? Who has made you feel as if you come first? Get curious about a time when this person extended themselves to you. Describe the scene. What were you feeling before their act? What were you feeling after? How can generosity transform a moment?

Because you are writing about a story you already know, see if you can learn something new about it in the writing of it now. What do you wonder about the interaction? Perhaps ask questions that help give you new insight into the person's actions or your response. Perhaps there is a metaphor in how the act has influenced you.

~

What Do We Owe the World?

Invitation to Read

"Show, don't tell," is common wisdom passed on to beginning writers, but I think "show *and* tell" is often more powerful in a poem. In "Figures" (79), Dorianne Laux creates a portrait of generosity using both specific details *and* insight into the giver's mindset and background. Laux's word choices in this poem set the scene well —*drunk, stumbling, rummage, stained, scraps*—but the poem also includes simple telling lines and questions that go to the heart of the poem. "Who can calculate the worth of one man's pain?" In the end, it's a stunning example of giving with no judgment, giving because giving is called for.

Invitation to Write

Think of someone you know who embodies generosity. What do they do? How do they do it? Do you have any insight into why they do what they do? Write a poem that is a portrait of their giving. Consider using both "show" and "tell." Consider, like Laux does in this poem, writing in third person. (It lends objectivity to the poem.) Play around with a title that might be a verb about how the person thinks.

OTHER POEMS THAT SPEAK TO GENEROSITY:

"Fused," Gloria Heffernan, 64.
"Remember," Rebecca Baggett, 80.
"When Giving Is All We Have," Alberto Ríos, 156.

TAKING CARE OF THE WORLD

How do we care for this planet that cares for us? Robin Wall Kimmerer says it this way in *Braiding Sweetgrass*: "Knowing that you love the earth changes you, activates you to defend and protect and celebrate. But when you feel that the earth loves you in return, that feeling transforms the relationship from a one-way street into a sacred bond."[9]

Writing poems is a way to explore and develop that "sacred bond." Consider writing poems that invite you to notice how the "earth loves you in return."

∼

Writing into the Sacred Bond

Invitation to Read

"Let's not muddy the water" is repeated again and again in "Water" by Sohrab Sepehri (71), translated from the Persian by Jerome W. Clinton. It's a powerful entreaty. To help motivate the reader's willingness to keep the water clean, the poet asks us to imagine multiple scenarios in which the stream we muddy might soon pass a tree, a bird, a woman, a community. Each stanza helps illuminate how interconnected all of life is—all these lives touching the same stream and how the stream is giving to each life. Each time the phrase "Let's not muddy the water" is repeated, it seems to gain in urgency.

Invitation to Write

Consider your relationship to water, air or earth. How do you care for it? And how does it care for you? Notice all it gives you— whether you are actively involved in caring for it or not.

Perhaps have a conversation with water, air or earth. Or write an epistolary poem, a thank you letter, acknowledging how the water (or air or earth) loves you.

~

Holding Ourselves Accountable

Invitation to Read

So much of our behavior stems from fear. In "Allowables" (81) by Nikki Giovanni, the speaker explores how she instinctively killed a spider, presumably a harmless one, for no reason except that she was afraid. The poem invites us to be very curious about our own subconscious and how fear informs our actions. The implications of the poem go far beyond killing a spider. When are we "allowed" to kill? When are we not? What is our responsibility to take care of other life forms, no matter our feelings toward them?

Invitation to Write

Think of a recent time when you took the life of another life form, no matter how small, be it mosquito, cockroach, spider, dandelion or rat. Be very curious. What was the life form you killed? Find out as much about it as you can. Wonder about its life and how its species might contribute to your own life in some grand scale. If you research it, is there anything admirable about this life form? Wonder about your instinct to kill. Where does it come from? When you consider it closely, what does it make you wonder about yourself? About what it is to be alive?

or

Think of a time when fear motivated you to do something. What choice did you not see in that moment? With utmost generosity toward yourself, speak to that frightened version of you. What do you know now that you did not know then?

ANOTHER POEM THAT SPEAKS TO TAKING CARE OF THE WORLD:

"A Valley Like This," William Stafford, 73.

HOW WE MIGHT MEET EACH OTHER

I once heard that in every interaction, we have a choice to meet other people in one of three ways: What we bring can be a minus, a zero, or a plus. A simple illustration: When meeting a stranger on the street, you can scowl at them, simply pass them by, or offer them a smile. This simple rubric has guided me in many interactions.

Writing poems can help us explore these three potential kinds of interactions in more complex ways. For instance, "Alien" by Lucy Griffith (88) explores both a plus and a minus in the same interaction. In "Neighbors" (78), James Crews shares many specific ideas about how we might choose to meet a moment with a plus.

∿

How to Meet Those in Grief

Invitation to Read

In a situation infused with sorrow, it is not always easy to know how to meet another person. Julia Spicher Kasdorf's "What I Learned

From My Mother" (76) speaks specifically to how to meet the grieving. It's basically a list of practical instructions—what to bring, what not to say. I appreciate that the poem explores both concrete actions and abstract ideas about how to be present to the bereaved, how to "offer healing." I also appreciate that instead of writing the poem in command form, Spicher Kasdorf repeats the phrase, "I learned _____." In this way, although the poem gives advice, it feels less like a lecture and more as if the poet is letting us in on a fabulous secret. It's a powerful, non-threatening way to frame a poem.

Invitation to Write

Think of someone you know who has positive ways to help those who grieve. Make a list of instructions based on things you've seen or heard them do. If they are still alive, consider having a conversation with them before you write. Ask them what they do, and why. If you don't have a conversation with them, simply think of past experience, observing them in action.

Consider using the same phrase that Spicher Kasdorf does: "I learned _____." In addition to what you learned, be curious about why this knowledge matters.

or

If you do not have a role model for how to meet people who are grieving in a sensitive way, then consider writing a poem about what you wish you could have learned on the subject. ("I wish I had learned how to _____," or "I wish I knew how to _____.") Who might have taught you but didn't, or couldn't? What would you be able to do now if you had had this wise person to offer you advice? How might this advice that you never got help you meet the present or a future moment differently?

～

Meeting the Unseen

Invitation to Read

So many people in our society go unseen, though "unseen" might be an overly polite way to say *ignored* or *disregarded*. How do we show up when we encounter others who might be very difficult for us to meet? And what is at stake in how we handle these moments?

In "For Everyone" (77), Elizabeth Brulé Farrell writes about an encounter with a man who is stoned and unable to care for himself. It's not a poem about how to help the man, it's a poem about how the speaker acknowledges her own thoughts about him. The poem explores the way she chooses to look at him, what she chooses to say, and how she says it. Because it is written in first person, the poem feels like an insight into someone else's process as they wrestle with their own judgment. It also feels like an invitation for us to do the same inner work as the poet has done.

Invitation to Write

Think about how you wish someone would meet you, especially if you are struggling. How do you wish they would look at you? What do you wish they might say or not say? How would they say it? What can you imagine would be the message inside the words, no matter which words are spoken? Write a poem in which you consider if you can speak this way to other people when they are struggling.

or

Think about a time when you were struggling and someone spoke to you in a way that made you feel deeply seen. What did they say with their body? With their words and tone? What was the response in you when you were met this way? How does it feel in your body when you remember the encounter now?

~

Remembering Each Other's Humanity

Invitation to Read

There are many instances when we don't treat each other as humans. Instead, we treat each other as a means to an end. In "Excuse Me" (87), MaryLisa DeDomenicis writes about a scene in a restaurant kitchen where the bus boy who does not speak English is referred to only as "the Mexican" and is treated very poorly by other workers who apparently do not speak his language. They don't even learn his name until the end of the poem. It's a portrait of disrespect, racism, and ongoing inhumanity, a small window into widespread callousness and cruelty.

Invitation to Write

Remember a time when you were treated not like a human but as a nameless being that existed only to fulfill someone else's needs. How did you remember your own humanity when other people did not? Or did you, too, forget your humanity? Was there someone else's voice in your head that helped you remember who you were? What would you say now about how you and other people should be treated? What do you know about yourself now that you didn't know then?

or

Write a poem to the bus boy. What questions do you have for him? How do you wish he had been treated? What emotions does his experience bring up in you? What language would you speak? What kind of body language might you use?

∾

OTHER POEMS THAT SPEAK TO HOW WE MIGHT MEET EACH OTHER:

"Shoulders," Naomi Shihab Nye, 43.
"The Dream's Wisdom," Marilyn Nelson, 75.
"Neighbors," James Crews, 78.
"Remember," Rebecca Baggett, 80.
"Alien," Lucy Griffith, 88.
"Every Mourning," Michael Kleber-Diggs, 90.
"Queens," Barbara Crooker, 94.
"The Pedicure," Annette Langlois Grunseth, 113.
"If You Knew," Ellen Bass, 114.
"Watching My Friend Pretend Her Heart Isn't Breaking,"
     Rosemerry Wahtola Trommer, 126.
"Death," Ron Starbuck, 133.

LEARNING TO SEE (RE-SEE) OURSELVES & EACH OTHER

"this is about more than color," writes Lucille Clifton in "the river between us" (84). She continues, "it is about how we learn to see ourselves." How do we learn to see ourselves? How do we learn to see each other? How do we meet in "the river between us" instead of standing on separate sides?

Reading poems is one way to learn about the lives and hearts of other people—to build compassion, understanding, empathy, genuineness and connection. And when we write honestly and vulnerably about our own experiences, we allow other people to see us, too.

Sometimes, as in the poems highlighted here, a poem also offers an insight into how we might expand our vision or clear our eyes so the heart might see other human beings and ourselves in new ways.

∾

Question Your Response

Invitation to Read

In "Black Boys Play the Classics" (86), Toi Derricotte depicts a scene in Penn Station where passersby, both black and white, are moved by three young black musicians. Most of the poem shows us what is happening on the surface, offering us details of how people respond to the musicians. We see the scene as if we're watching a movie. But the last four lines of the poem ask us to look at what is driving the scene. Derricotte's ending emulates a multiple-choice quiz. Because the poet doesn't offer an answer, the readers themselves must choose between the opposites the poet suggests. It's an invitation to notice bias, to question what is at the core of our "trembling."

Invitation to Write

Consider the multiple-choice question in Toi Derricotte's poem. What did you notice about your own response to the scene in "Black Boys Play the Classics" *before* you got to the end? What do you notice about how you responded to Derricotte's question? Let yourself be curious about your answers. Write honestly about your responses. What in your upbringing and life experience might have led you to answer the way you did?

∽

What's the Pebble in Your Shoe?

Invitation to Read

How is it that humans can normalize war? How is it that we can go about our days, brushing our teeth and fixing our car and drinking coffee and going to work, while other humans are being bombed, shot at, treated unjustly?

In "Normal" (97), Reginald Harris compares the way we become accustomed to walking with the pain of a pebble in our shoe to how we become accustomed to living with a much greater pain—the pain of other humans suffering and being killed. How do we wake ourselves up? Sometimes the words of another person shake us up, as in this poem; twice, someone else says something that makes the speaker of the poem aware there is a problem. Twice, Harris asks, "then what do you do?" The question goes unanswered on the page, letting it live in the reader. When you realize you can do something about the pain, or not, what do you do?

Invitation to Write

In effect, Reginald Harris's poem is the "someone" who asks you to remember "there *is* a war still going on." Now that you remember, answer Harris's question: "What do you do?" Write a response.

or

What atrocity in the world has become a "pebble in your shoe"? Whose pain do you choose not to see daily? Take a moment, or an hour, or half a day, and immerse yourself in the story of another's pain. Write about this experience—of opening to someone you've been choosing not to see. What do you learn about them? What do you learn about yourself in this process of choosing to see their lives and know their suffering? If arriving at answers is difficult, then find questions and ask them.

~

Honoring Those Who See What We Don't

Invitation to Read

Perhaps you know someone who can make a delicious meal out of what looked like scraps meant for compost and trash. In "Ribollita" (151), Donna Hilbert praises another person who looks at a tough rind of cheese and vegetables at the edge of spoilage and sees the potential for a warm bowl of savory soup. The poem is a celebration of someone who can look past the surface and nourish other people because of this ability. It's a sweetly meta process—just by noticing that someone else sees differently than we do, it allows us to see differently, too.

Invitation to Write

Think of someone who has a world view you admire. It could be someone from the news, someone from history, or someone you know personally. Try to think of a specific time when their perspective brought about a positive change. Be curious about their vision. Write a praise poem for that person, describing what they could see that other people could not. Write about what you learn about yourself as you explore how they see the world.

OTHER POEMS THAT SPEAK TO HOW WE LEARN TO SEE (RE-SEE) OURSELVES AND EACH OTHER:

"Adolescent," Teddy Macker, 82.
"the river between us," Lucille Clifton, 84.
"Halal Delicatessen," Patrick Hicks, 96.
"Champion the Enemy's Need," Kim Stafford, 101.

ENTERING THE BIG
CONVERSATION

I began this book by asking you to consider these prompts as invitations to enter "the big conversation" of what it means to be alive, adding your voice to the voices of every other poet and writer and artist around the world, over all time. Sometimes I'm aware of feeling unworthy of joining this exchange, and sometimes I feel my voice isn't welcome. And yet the invitation to enter dialogue with the world still stands. Our silence, too, is a part of this conversation.

∿

When Our Voices Are Unwelcome

Invitation to Read

There are times when other people make it known that they are not only disinterested in hearing our voice, they feel hostility and animosity toward it,. Claudia Rankine writes about such a scenario in "Untitled" (85), in which the speaker of the poem is about to enter a conference room, then hears two men speaking derogatorily about "being around black people." Because the poem is written in second person, it feels as if you, the reader, are the one overhearing the conversation. And now you have a choice.

Invitation to Write

Respond to the poem. How do you feel about entering the room with these men and their bigotry? How do you enter a conversation knowing that certain voices, including yours, are not welcome in the conversation? Or do you choose not to enter?

or

Remember a time, past or present, when you felt your voice was not welcome. What effect did this have on you? What did you do or not do? Looking back at that moment, what do you know now that you didn't know then? What new questions do you have about that moment?

or

Write an epistolary poem, a letter to yourself, that wonders about your voice in the big conversation. Perhaps it is a letter of encouragement. Perhaps it is a letter of celebration. Perhaps you have advice for yourself. Perhaps you have questions for yourself about what obstacles you face, what fears come up, or what dreams you have.

~

The Word in Everyone's Mouths

Invitation to Read

Sometimes a single word is all it takes to realize that we are in conversation with every other person on the planet. That idea is at the heart of "The Word That Is a Prayer" by Ellery Akers (155). The poem begins as a list of people who, even in this moment, might be saying "please." In the first line, the poem suggests that you, too, are one of these people. All of us are linked by this single word. The second half of the poem is a musing on the word *please*, both sonically and metaphorically. Akers compares the word first to a feather that floats up, then as weather that comes down and surrounds us all, connects us all. The poem is a potent exploration of how a single, simple word illumines our common humanity. But even more, it's an invitation to see how we are surrounded by everyone else's prayers—as they are by ours. What is our responsibility to each other? How do we respond?

Invitation to Write

Imagine in this moment that you can hear every single *please* being said in the world. What is it like? How does it feel? How do the words move around you? Where do they land? What do you notice about your body? What do you notice about the sound of your own *please?*

or

Think of a word or phrase you say often. Imagine who else in the world might say that phrase, too. Perhaps list a few of these people. How does your common use of this phrase unite you? Imagine that these other people could hear you or intuit you, too, as you say it. Be curious about the word or phrase itself. Perhaps come up with a metaphor for how it works in the world after it has left your mouth.

ANOTHER POEM THAT SPEAKS TO ENTERING THE BIG CONVERSATION:

Untitled (You're invited to visit), Gregory Orr, 25.

HOW WE MIGHT BRIDGE THE DISCONNECT

There are so many moments when we might feel "othered"—moments when, because of race or gender or political beliefs or religious convictions or citizenship, we find ourselves at the heart of conflict and disconnection. What then? How do poems help us explore these feelings of division? What part of you is interested in ways we might come together? What part of you resists this possibility?

～

Envision What Is Possible

Invitation to Read

"And I want to shout, *Morning!*" writes Michael Kleber-Diggs in his poem "Every Mourning" (90). But the speaker in the poem does not do this. Instead, a morning walk becomes the backdrop for an interaction that causes the speaker of the poem to "retreat into myself as far as I can." This poem is powerful both in the way it shows the pain of division and racism and in the way it imagines what else is possible.

At the center of the poem, the speaker ponders how ants work together. "I want . . . to carry the weight of the day together," writes Kleber-Diggs. "I want to be part of a colony where I feel easy walking around." It is at this very moment that a "fellow traveler" crosses the street, ostensibly to avoid encountering the speaker of the poem. I admire how the poet can weave a positive, constructive way that humans might interact into the exact moment when a morning becomes a reason (as the title suggests) for "mourning."

Invitation to Write

At the heart of Kleber-Diggs's poem is the metaphor of an ant colony and how the ants seem able to do what all humans can't yet do: work together to build something "sturdier and grander." Think of an example in the natural world where a community of animals, insects or plants work together in service of their mutual well-being. Use it as a model to wonder how humans, too, might learn to live and work together.

~

What It Looks Like When We Work Together

Invitation to Read

In "House of Mercury" (93), Fady Joudah writes about a storm that damages a home and yard, and then how people of different races and generations come together to help tend to what has been uprooted and torn apart. Though it's a story of destruction, it's also a story of connection, "fear that comes to nothing," and the surprise blessings that sometimes arise from challenges. Poems such as "House of Mercury" essentially build new neural pathways in the collective brain, a pathway that says "This is what it can look like."

Invitation to Write

Write about a time when people of very different backgrounds came together for a common positive purpose. Be curious about what that moment from the past has to say to you in this moment. How has it informed you?

~

Get to Know the Other

Invitation to Read

The title of Kim Stafford's poem "Champion the Enemy's Need" (101) contains a fabulous paradox. Can you be a hero who fights for your enemy?

The poem itself is written in command form, offering the reader instructions. Though the poem is quite short, each line offers a small bridge for how to create a connection with someone who is theoretically not on your side. The instructions themselves are simple and feel doable. They touch on the basic needs of all humans and show how "our enemy" has all the same needs as we do.

Invitation to Write

Think of someone with whom you struggle—either an individual person or a group of people. Imagine that you are asked not just to care for this person/these people, but to be their *champion*. What will you ask them? How would you hope that you would treat them? Give your instructions on how to be your best self as you meet "your enemy." What actions are asked of you? What changes of heart might be necessary?

❧

OTHER POEMS THAT SPEAK TO HOW WE MIGHT BRIDGE THE DISCONNECT:

"Phase One," Dilruba Ahmed, 39.
"Alien," Lucy Griffith, 88.
"Forgiveness," Christen Careaga, 91.
"Halal Delicatessen," Patrick Hicks, 96.
"Detour," Ruth Feldman, 146.

IMAGINE PEACE, CREATE POSITIVE CHANGE

One of the books that most changed the way I speak is *Don't Think of an Elephant* by George Lakoff.[10] In it, he explains the neurolinguistic principles of framing that determine our thoughts. Especially interesting to me is how each time we say something in the negative, we reinforce that frame, even though it is the opposite of what we want. For instance, if I say, "Don't think of an elephant," I've subverted my desired outcome. Why? First, the brain processes "think of an elephant," then it processes "don't." The elephant is already there.

Why does this matter? I would suggest that part of our work as poets is to help visualize the world we most want to inhabit. I think of the phrase "Poets against the war." The intention is admirable, of course, but notice how the phrasing reinforces the idea of war. In contrast, "poets for peace" establishes *peace* as the dominant framework.

It can be harder to dream of what is possible than to rail against what we do not want. The poems in this section do that hard work and perhaps inspire us to do the same.

∼

What Will You Do for Peace?

Invitation to Read

I am drawn to the magical thinking of Rafael Jesús González in "Origami Crane Tanka / *Tanka de grulla Origami*" (109). The poem is built on an "if/then" statement in which the poet pledges himself to a lifelong task in the name of peace. Though it seems scientifically improbable that folding paper cranes could make a wish come true, the strength of the poem is its devotion to peace and the poet's willingness to work for it "for the rest of my days." That passion feels *exactly* like what it takes to work "magic," to make real change, to create peace.

Invitation to Write

What are you willing to do for peace? Perhaps consider including something playful and magical about how wishes come true. If your wish for peace did come true, what might that peace look like? Magic notwithstanding, what else can you imagine doing in the name of peace? Write a list poem of many ideas, or explore one idea deeply.

∼

Begin with the Self

Invitation to Read

Sometimes in our wish to create positive change, we dream so big that we set ourselves up for an impossible task. But in "Clearing" (110), Martha Postlethwaite invites us to take the only first step we can really take: to start with ourselves. The predominant metaphor for the poem, creating "a clearing in the dense forest of your life," suggests that if we find an inner spaciousness, we have a better chance of finding clarity about what gifts we have to offer. The poem itself is spare—only a few words per line, and it seems to model the spaciousness it promotes.

Invitation to Write

Imagine doing what this poem suggests. Perhaps go to a real clearing in the woods, or perhaps find a seat in your own home, close your eyes and go to an inner clearing. Perhaps cup your hands and hold them out, as Postlethwaite suggests. What arrives? Anything? Are you aware of what you wish might arrive? Are you frightened or resistant to what actually arrives? If nothing arrives, how does that feel? How long do you wait for something to arrive? Are you willing to wait in the clearing again? Perhaps begin your writing with, "I sat in the clearing with my hands open and _____."

∿

OTHER POEMS THAT SPEAK TO IMAGINING PEACE AND CREATING POSITIVE CHANGE:

"Passing the Orange," Leo Dangel, 50.
"Your Birthday," Pat Schneider, 99.
"Champion the Enemy's Need," Kim Stafford, 101.
"My Species," Jane Hirshfield, 108.
"Some Advice for Clearing Brush," Jeff Coomer, 111.

MEETING THE PAIN OF THE WORLD

"The heart that breaks open can contain the whole universe," says environmental activist and author Joanna Macy. "Your heart is that large. Trust it."[11] Of course, it hurts when the heart breaks open. Who would ask for such a breaking?

But oh, the gifts of opening. Poetry is ever ready to receive a broken heart—the blank page is ever open to meet what might feel impossible. The poems in this section touch on unthinkable events with such vulnerability, such tenderness, such ferocity, that they make me believe Macy's words.

❧

Write the Impossible Letter

Invitation to Read

What could you possibly say to the parents of a child whose life was taken by your child? This is the premise of "For the Man Whose Son My Son Killed" by Gary Earl Ross (102). This epistolary poem is filled with love for a child, with revelation spawned by hearing another's pain, with agony for senseless loss, and with respect for other parents. It ends with an apology that feels saturated with truth. It's a poem that touches an impossible grief to reconcile—the death of a child—and instead of turning away from the pain, it steps toward it with open hands, open heart.

Invitation to Write

Think of someone who has been hurt in a deep, soul-gutting way by you or by someone you love. Feel into the other person's pain. As much as you can, put yourself in their situation. Write them an apology poem, knowing you need not send it or show it to anyone. Be as honest as you can about your actions. Notice the effect in your body when you take responsibility. Notice the effect when you say you are sorry.

~

Caring for the Compassionate Self

Invitation to Read

When other people are harmed or killed, it can be excruciating to experience their loss. The pain of that loss can be compounded when we (or someone else) try to rationalize the death. How, then, do we heal?

Thich Nhat Hanh's poem "For Warmth" (104), written after the American bombing of Ben Tre during the Vietnam War, is a description of how the speaker of the poem responded when the heart was already broken open. Though the central action itself is simple, "I hold my face in my two hands," the rest of the poem is a portrait of what is unseen inside this action. The poem allows us to see both the external portrayal and the internal landscape of the speaker. What is not seen, but what the poem tells, is how the speaker is meeting a spectrum of feelings that are present.

Invitation to Write

Think of a time when you have let yourself feel deeply into another's pain. Where were you? What was the circumstance? Write a poem that is a self-portrait showing two things:

1. What the scene might have looked like to anyone who was watching as you processed this pain
2. What was happening inside you that no one else could see

Perhaps write in third person—sometimes it is easier to meet these very difficult moments when we speak of ourselves as a she, he, or they, allowing ourselves to be witnesses of our pain instead of reporting or feeling it directly. Perhaps use these phrases: "If you had seen her, you would have seen _____. What you could not have seen was _____."

∽

OTHER POEMS THAT SPEAK TO MEETING THE PAIN OF THE WORLD:

"Nor'easter," James Crews, 74.
"Breathe," Lynn Ungar, 105.

HONORING THE BODY

What is your experience in your body right now? Is it in pain? Are you critical of your body? Are you grateful for your body? Does it feel good? Are you accepting of some parts and not others? Do you feel connected to your body? Or, are you like James Joyce's character Mr. Duffy, who "lived a short distance from his body"?[12] Do you let thoughts of your body take over your other thoughts? If your body could speak, what would it say to you? Oh, the relationship with the body . . . it is one of our most intimate of all relationships —a relationship that is so important to explore!

∾

Who Else Lives in Your "Bone-House"?

Invitation to Read

In "Walking with My Delaware Grandfather" (117) Denise Low speaks to how the presence of our ancestors can be present with us in our bodies, or as she says, in "the bone-house where my heart beats." The speaker of the poem honors how her grandfather (and his mother through him) are alive in her now, invoking memories of things they said and did. The sense of how the speaker embodies a legacy comes through in the final line: "His blood still pulses through this hand."

Invitation to Write

In what ways do you sense that your ancestors live in your body? Do you have a shared physical trait, like Low's cleft in her chin that she shares with her grandfather? Or a shared sense of humor? A similar way of seeing the world? Or are you aware of how they might argue with you or challenge you in some way? When are you most aware of them? When do you forget? How do they remind you they are there?

~

Praising an Unsung Part of the Body

Invitation to Read

We take so much for granted with our bodies. There are bones most of us can't name, organs we don't really understand what they do, processes we barely comprehend. In "About Standing (in Kinship)" (119), Kimberly M. Blaeser shares some of the intricacies of the foot and how the bones work together to allow us to stand. "Maybe we should give more honor to feet," she writes—then uses the elegant structure of the foot as a metaphor to honor human connections, too, and how we rely on each other. The body has so much to teach us about how life works across scale, and, as Blaeser suggests, it has something to teach us about our commonality.

Invitation to Write

Choose a body part you don't understand well. Your spleen? Your amygdala? Or perhaps choose a body part that you are struggling with. Research it. Learn how it works, what it does for the rest of the body. What does this body part have to teach you about what it is to be alive? If it could give you advice about how to treat other people, what would it say?

∾

The Fullness That Comes with Sacrifice

Invitation to Read

Sometimes when we meet a challenge with our body, it can heighten our awareness of our aliveness. Such is the case in "New Bathing Suit" (123) when Terri Kirby Erickson honors a friend who has had a mastectomy. "There is no one more alive than she is now," Kirby Erickson writes, observing how her friend moves through a swimming pool, celebrating what her body can do. Though a part of the friend's body has been removed, Kirby Erickson finds ways that her friend, paradoxically, is even more present than before, fueled with "the fullness that comes to us, with sacrifice."

Invitation to Write

Write a poem about someone (perhaps even you) whose body carries a scar that tells a story of survival. What is the story behind that scar? Is it seen or hidden? What do you notice about their body now —how it works, how it lives, how it continues to carry a soul? Describe something they can do in their body. How does that body move through the world? Is it possible the person is brought more to life through the healing of their wound? Or through the acceptance of their wound?

OTHER POEMS THAT SPEAK TO HONORING THE BODY:

"The Pedicure," Annette Langlois Grunseth, 113.
"Sponge Bath," Terri Kirby Erickson, 115.
"Living in the Body," Joyce Sutphen, 116.

MET WITH SURPRISE DELIGHT

Sometimes when we least expect it, we are met with joy. Perhaps it's a bizarre event, as in "Potatoes" by Lucy Adkins (152). Perhaps it's an encounter with an animal, another human or even a startling fact that somehow opens our eyes to the wonder of life. Once we've been met by wonder, there's something powerful about writing into that experience—not only because it memorializes the delight, but because as we explore this kind of moment, often it continues to unfold for us in new ways.

∽

Trying on New Perspectives

Invitation to Read

I am often startled into wonder by facts about other living plants and animals. This is the premise of Danusha Laméris' poem "Feeding the Worms" (137), in which the poet begins with a surprising detail about the taste buds of earthworms and how they literally take in the world. It's a poem that teaches us, but it also reveals how when we better understand another creature, it can change the way we interact with them.

There's so much pleasure in this poem—of discovery, of engagement—and then, oh! The last line opens the whole poem into a reflection on our own mortality. What are the moments of delight we might take in before we die? How might we find pleasure in the ways we nourish the world and ourselves?

Invitation to Write

Choose any animal or insect that lives near you—an animal you are likely to encounter at some point in a year. You need not like this animal. Research it. What do you learn about this animal that surprises you? Delights you?

Choose one or more facts and write about them. What does this animal have to teach you about what it is to live, or to die? How might you meet this animal differently, next time you come across it?

❧

A Small Spasm of Joy

Invitation to Read

"Why am I not allowed delight?" asks Ada Limón, the question at the heart of "Give Me This" (138). The poem details a surprise encounter with a groundhog. And though the small animal is pilfering homegrown tomatoes, and though the speaker in the poem has been asked to think on suffering, this scene elicits in the speaker "a small spasm of joy" as the groundhog finds pleasure in devouring the juicy tomatoes.

As a reader, the speaker's joy comes as a bit of a shock. You're not mad? You don't try to shoo the groundhog from the garden? It's thrilling, really, this unexpected turn of events—and the poem incites in *me* an unpredicted, small spasm of joy. *Why not delight?* The poem invites us to find joy in the world as it is—to revel in whatever surprises a day might offer us.

Invitation to Write

What has recently brought you surprise joy? Recall the scene. What were you feeling before that moment? Why did the joy surprise you? How did it inform the rest of the day? What did it teach you about surviving?

OTHER POEMS THAT SPEAK TO SURPRISE DELIGHT:

"U Pick," Barbara Crooker, 139.
"Potatoes," Lucy Adkins, 152.

EXPLORING KINDNESS

It can be so small, the gesture that changes everything. A wave. A smile. A touch. A few words. At its foundation, kindness conveys connection. A kind act says, *you belong*. It says, *I see you*. It says, *there is good in the world*. I am always astonished at how just hearing about an act of kindness between people I don't even know can move me to tears and make me grateful to be alive—a good reason to write and share kindness poems! Another good reason: when we explore kindness in writing, it can have a calming effect on our minds and bring us into a more receptive, open state.

~

These Fleeting Temples

Invitation to Read

In every interaction, there is an opportunity for kindness—at the store, in our homes, at work, on the street. In "Small Kindnesses" (142), Danusha Laméris begins the poem by listing many specific examples—things people say, things people do. The end of the poem is more of a musing on moments of kindness—why these moments are important, perhaps now more than ever. She asks, "What if they are the true dwelling of the holy, these fleeting temples we make together"? It's a powerful question that invites us to wonder what is really at stake with our interactions.

Invitation to Write

Make a list of small interactions, "fleeting temples we make together," that show how kindness might play out in daily ways. Perhaps choose examples that have happened to you in recent days. What effect(s) did these acts have on you? At the time, where did you feel a response in your body? Writing about those acts of kindness now, what do you notice about your body? What questions do you have about how kindness works? Ask these questions with no need to answer them.

~

How We Save Each Other

Invitation to Read

Kindness is almost always a blessing, but *especially* when we find ourselves in need of help from strangers—for instance, when it's getting dark and our car battery has died. This is the scenario for Alison Luterman's poem "Jump" (154), in which she meets multiple people who extend kindness. Part of the joy of this poem is in noting that even the best intentions sometimes don't have the desired consequences—but they are no less kind. Also worth noting: sometimes the person who "saves" us needs saving. And so it is that this web of kindnesses is complex, yet also so simple, like a "spark arcing quicker than thought.

Invitation to Write

"Your legacy is every life you touched," Maya Angelou once said to Oprah Winfrey.[13] It's true for all of us. Think of a time when you needed kindness and someone else stepped in to help you. How is your life a legacy of that person's kindness? What might have happened without that kindness? How did it feel to ask for kindness? What did you learn from that moment? Is there a way you gave back to the person who helped you? How do you carry on that legacy of kindness? Or how do you not?

∾

OTHER POEMS THAT SPEAK TO EXPLORING KINDNESS:

"Neighbors," James Crews, 78.
"Why I Smile at Strangers," Rosemerry Wahtola Trommer, 143.
"The Aunty Poem (Mi Privilege Es Tu Privilege)," Mohja
    Kahf, 144.
"Shine," Julie Cadwallader Staub, 160.

REMEMBERING THE PANDEMIC

The pandemic changed so much—how we greet each other, how we meet each other, how we work, how we play, how we touch or don't touch, what we wear, how we move. There were huge losses—loved ones, careers, homes. And there were, for each of us, thousands of smaller losses—celebrations, vacations, events, goals, connections with family and friends, social rituals.

The pandemic also brought some silver linings and blessings—for some people, a connection with silence, with solitude, with not doing, with stillness. For others, a sense of community, and appreciation for life, an appreciation for caregivers, the satisfaction that comes from helping.

Writing poems about the pandemic can help us name our griefs, name our blessings, and honor how our lives have been shaped by this global experience.

～

Dear 2020

Invitation to Read

Some of the poems in this book were written during the pandemic. Now that you have a little distance from the onset of COVID-19, how has time changed your perspective on that crisis?

Invitation to Write

One idea for reflecting on the pandemic is to simply write a poem letter. Perhaps you begin, "Dear 2020." Or maybe "Dear COVID." Or perhaps, "Dear Time of the Pandemic." Perhaps notice what your expectations were at the beginning of the pandemic and how they changed. Perhaps honor loss. Perhaps notice what blessings from that time are still with you. What will never be the same? What didn't change?

∼

What Do You Want to Remember?

Invitation to Read

In "when we get through this" (165), Maya Stein offers the reader a detail-rich inventory of important lessons and beautiful transformations that happened during the pandemic. Stein relates how many people told stories, showed up for each other and themselves, and changed their perspective to be more global, more generous, more kind. Stein ends the poem with a powerful wish: "I want us to remember this and to keep remembering." What do you want to remember?

Invitation to Write

What lessons did the pandemic teach you? In what ways are you still attentive to these lessons? What have you forgotten? What did you know in those first days or months or years of the pandemic that you would like to have at the forefront of your thoughts now? Perhaps begin with these words: "I want to remember_____."

~

OTHER POEMS THAT SPEAK TO THE PANDEMIC:

"In the Third Month of the Pandemic, My Husband Goes Through
    His Sock Drawer," Holly J. Hughes, 36.
"Sheltered in Place," Richard Levine, 46.
"Pandemic," Lynn Ungar, 161.
"Love and Fear in a Pandemic," Christine Stewart-Nuñez, 162.
"A few days after my first vaccine," Alison Luterman, 164.

WHEN EVERYONE FINDS THEIR
WAY BACK TOGETHER

Sometimes we can feel so distant from each other, so disconnected, so lost, so far from home. And when we feel communion, unity, connection—oh, how it fills us! In "The Story Wheel" by Joy Harjo (145), the poet describes a welcome home dance in which "everyone finds their way back together." How does this happen? How do we find our way "back together"—in our families, in our communities, as a people?

One path to reconnection is through telling and listening to each other's stories. This is one of the great gifts offered us by books such as *Poetry of Presence II*—the weaving of the voices and experiences of so many, helping us come together. As Mark Nepo invites us in "A Pearl of Wind" (168): "So sing me a song. For yourself, but let me listen."

∿

Dancing Across the Distance

Invitation to Read

It can be very difficult to even imagine "coming back together" with other people when we have been deeply hurt. Of course, the body remembers pain. Of course, the heart does not want to be hurt again. But oh, the beauty and peace possible when we do come back together!

In his poem "The Distance / *La Distancia*" (148 / 149), Rafael Jesús González invites us to see this process of coming together as a "pilgrimage" and the space between us as "holy ground." It's a powerful reframing of this journey toward connection. In his description, those who are making this pilgrimage do so with vulnerability and joy, and the steps they take across the distance light the way for other people to come, too.

Invitation to Write

Imagine you are following in the light-filled steps of those who have already made the pilgrimage described in "The Distance / *La Distancia*." What is it like to traverse this terrain toward other people in a new way? Who are these other people? Family? Strangers? Friends? Enemies? How does it feel in your body as you move through the new terrain? What sounds can you imagine hearing?

or

How would you like to make the "pilgrimage" that connects you with other humans? How do you envision that space between you? What would make you want to cross that distance? Who do you wish would meet you in this space? Describe your body—what do you do with your arms, your legs, your face? How do you wish you could move toward others?

~

Learning to Trust

Invitation to Read

Coming together with other people requires an enormous amount of trust. But how do we develop this trust? In part, perhaps, it comes from seeing all the small ways we already trust each other and the world.

In "Trust" (153), when Thomas R. Smith describes how even taking a car to a new mechanic is a form of trust, he invites us to see how much confidence in others it takes just to get through a day. Even putting an envelope in the mail involves a small leap of faith. It is the details in this poem that open a door to mindfulness and trust. We see through Smith's specifics what choices are being made by the speaker. In each moment, we must ask, "Do I dare trust now?"

In the third stanza, Smith opens our idea of trust by speaking not only of the human world, but of the natural world, too, suggesting perhaps that it is life itself that we are learning to trust— that the wind and the water are doing exactly what they are meant to do. And then, in the final couplet, comes an almost startling invitation: can we trust that our lives are happening exactly as they are meant to, though we have no idea where we might end up?

Invitation to Write

Think about your day so far. What small choices have you made that involved trust? Trust that the sun is still burning at the center of our solar system? Trust that your legs will carry you across the room? Trust that you have a voice worth exploring?

Make a list of things you trust in this moment. How does exploring this list affect you? What daily tasks might transform into small acts of building trust with the world?

∾

Making "Something Greater from the Difference"

Invitation to Read

Poetry can be a recalibration—not toward our goals, but toward our life. In "When Giving Is All We Have" (156), Alberto Ríos explores the communion of giving—why we give, how we give, and what transformations might happen when we come together and give of ourselves. The poem is simple in its language and syntax, yet it seems to touch the very heart of the mystery of what it means to be alive. Like life itself, the poem is full of paradox. Like life itself, the poem reaches toward opposites. It honors differences, and it calls on us to bring what we have, to bring what do not have, to receive from other people what they have to offer, and to make "something greater from the difference."

Invitation to Write

Write a list that begins "I want to give you ____." It might be very interesting to explore why you want to give these things. What drives you to give? What is it in you that calls you to be in service to other beings? Try to not know the answer when you start writing. Be very curious about what comes up.

or

What has been given to you? Who has given it? How has their gift in you, matched with the gifts you offer, become "something greater"?

∾

OTHER POEMS THAT SPEAK TO EVERYONE FINDING THEIR WAY BACK TOGETHER:

ENDNOTES

1. *Poetry of Presence II: An Anthology of Mindfulness Poems,* edited by Phyllis Cole-Dai and Ruby Wilson (Grayson Books, 2023).

2. *Exploring Poetry of Presence: A Companion Guide for Readers, Writers & Workshop Facilitators* by Gloria Heffernan (Back Porch Productions, 2021).

3. Joi Sharp can be found at http://joisharp.com/.

4. Kim Rosen quote used with permission.

5. "Breaking the Fast" by Naomi Shihab Nye from *Red Suitcase* (BOA Editions, 1994).

6. Ram Dass in conversation with Raghu Markus, from "What is the Ultimate Act of Compassion" on the Ram Dass Foundation website: https://rb.gy/p6ecpl.

7. "Messenger" by Mary Oliver from *Thirst* (Beacon Press, 2007).

8. *Wake Up Grateful: The Transformative Practice of Taking Nothing for Granted* by Kristi Nelson (Storey Publishing, 2020).

9. *Braiding Sweetgrass: Indigenous Wisdom, Scientific Knowledge, and the Teachings of Plants* by Robin Wall Kimmerer (Milkweed Editions, 2013).

10. *Don't Think of an Elephant: Know Your Values and Frame the Debate* by George Lakoff (Chelsea Green Publishing, 2004).

11. *Despair and Personal Power in the Nuclear Age* by Joanna Macy (New Society Publishers, 1983).

12. *Dubliners* (Bantam Classics, 1990).

13. Maya Angelou in conversation with Oprah Winfrey, related in Oprah Winfrey's commencement address to Agnes Scott College (Atlanta, GA, May 13, 2017).

BOUQUET OF GRATEFULNESSES

Thank you to all the poets in *Poetry of Presence II*. I feel so lucky, so grateful to read your words and to feel into your poems. Thank you for the conversations you've started. It is my hope that I have honored your poems.

Thank you to Ruby R. Wilson and Phyllis Cole-Dai for your hard work and open hearts, for being in service to poetry and mindfulness. What a gift you have given me and so many with both *Poetry of Presence* volumes!

Thank you to Paula Lepp *(doo doo do do do doo)*, this book's first reader, for your keen eyes, quick mind, thoughtfulness and attentiveness. I think I'm a bunny.

Thank you to Joi Sharp for years and years of satsang, for inspiring me to open, to fall in love with presence.

Thank you to Eric and Vivian for all the ways you've carried me with your love and support. You are incredible.

ABOUT THE AUTHOR

Rosemerry Wahtola Trommer lives on the banks of the wild San Miguel River in southwest Colorado with her husband and daughter. She co-hosts Emerging Form (a podcast on creative process), Secret Agents of Change (a surreptitious kindness cabal) and Soul Writer's Circle. Her poetry has appeared on *A Prairie Home Companion*, *PBS News Hour*, *O Magazine*, *American Life in Poetry*, on Carnegie Hall stage, and on river rocks she leaves around town. Her collection *Hush* won the Halcyon Prize. *Naked for Tea* was a finalist for the Able Muse Book Award. Her most recent collection is *All the Honey*. She believes in practice, and since 2006, she has written a poem a day. These can be read on her blog, *A Hundred Falling Veils*. Her daily audio series, *The Poetic Path*, can be found on the Ritual app. Other passions include gardening, hiking, Nordic skiing, singing and walking in the dark. One-word mantra: Adjust. Three-word mantra: I'm still learning.

ABOUT THE AUTHOR

SELECTED BOOKS

BY ROSEMERRY WAHTOLA TROMMER

All the Honey (Samara Press, 2023)

Beneath All Appearances: An Unwavering Peace, with Rashani Réa and Damascena Tanis (Sacred Spiral Press, 2023)

Hush: Poems (Middle Creek Publishing, 2020)

Naked for Tea (Able Muse, 2018)

Even Now (Lithic Press, 2016)

The Less I Hold (Turkey Buzzard Press, 2012)

The Miracle Already Happening: Everyday Life with Rumi (Liquid Light Press, 2011)

Intimate Landscape: The Four Corners in Poetry & Photography (Durango Herald Small Press, 2009)

Holding Three Things at Once (Turkey Buzzard Press, 2008)

Insatiable: Poems (Sisu Press, 2004)

If You Listen: Poems & Photographs of the San Juan Mountains (Western Reflections Press, 2000)

Complete the collection.

Poetry of Presence
An Anthology of Mindfulness Poems

Phyllis Cole-Dai & Ruby Wilson, editors

A popular anthology of more than 150 mindfulness poems, mostly by contemporary or recent poets, both acclaimed and lesser known. These poems call us to the Here and Now, and help us to dwell there. The Here and Now is all that truly belongs to us, and as the poets say, it's enough.

"If you choose one anthology, I say let it be this one for the amazement— for the voices that, surprisingly, will speak to what you want to find in yourself."
> —*Grace Cavalieri, host and producer, "The Poet and the Poem from the Library of Congress"*

You may also be interested in

Exploring Poetry of Presence
A Companion Guide for Readers, Writers, & Workshop Facilitators
Gloria Heffernan

Enrich your experience of the original *Poetry of Presence* collection with this able guide through its wondrous terrain. Perfect for individual and/or group use. Includes eight engaging reading strategies, fifty stimulating writing prompts, and a twelve-week workshop curriculum.

Available through your favorite bookstore